The Spiralizer Cookbootk

Quick and Delicious Spiralizer Recipes Made Simple

Brandon Mitchell

TABLE OF CONTENTS

INTRODUCTION

Whether you have a hand-held spiralizer, an electric one, or you have just bought yourself an affordable stand spiralizer, I am sure that you can agree with me on this one – this revolutionary kitchen appliance is really life-changing.

Once this magical appliance has hit the market, sold for an inexpensive price, most of us forever said farewell to shredding cabbages and peeling and chopping veggies for salads. Spiralizing vegetables in a single motion, the spiralizer has brought cooking to a whole different level.

If your kitchen is decorated with a shiny spiralizer and you do not use this appliance for anything besides zucchini noodles and carrot salads, it is time to turn your spiralizer into something more than a mere decoration.

Useful for any kind of meal, whether breakfast dishes, salads, soups, rice, or even desserts, it is almost a sin to use the spiralizer only for zucchini noodles.

Offering you 100 different ways in which you can use your spiralizer, and 100 delightful recipes to satisfy your belly and cravings, this books is the ultimate spiralizer cookbook you will ever find.

THE SPIRAL JOURNEY

No matter how fancy (or not!) your spiralizer model is, it is good at one thing – spiralizing vegetables. This cookbook does not have favorite models, nor will try to convince you to pick one over another. No. This book puts its sole focus on the spiralized veggies and what you can use your spiralizer for. Okay, I might also share a few tips that will help you master the art of spiralizing, as well.

So, let's get started.

THE ART OF SPIRALIZING

First things first, let's explain what spiralizing is. Spiralizing is a process of transforming plain vegetables into something unique, fun, and creative. Spiralizing means turning the veggies into noodles. It really is as simple as that, but that simplicity is also super revolutionary. There are tons of different ways in which you can cook with veggie noodles.

Pasta

The first and most common way is for making healthy pasta. If you follow a gluten-free, ketogenic, paleo, low carb, or vegan diet, then you know how hard it is to choose a salad over spaghetti at a restaurant. But who says it has to be that way?

By choosing a healthy diet and go against the grains, you will pack yourself with beneficial nutrients that will improve your overall health. And if you are worried about your hungry tummy, you don't have a reason for it. The veggie noodles are not only fun to make and nutritious, but they are super filling as well. You can top them with whatever sauce you feel in the mood for, and transform any pasta bowl into a healthier and low carb meal that will neither spike your blood sugar, nor will make you fat.

Salads

Cooking in this busy and fast-paced world can sometimes be a challenge. Who has the time for shredding or chopping veggies when there are so many other things to do as well. If you skip your salads just because you don't have time to assemble them, then let your spiralizer do all the work for you. Providing you with a full bowl of spiralized vegetables in a jiffy, the spiralizer will show you that making salads has never been neither quicker nor more convenient.

Rice

Again, if you follow a low carb or gluten free diet, then you probably know how challenging skipping or replacing rice can really be. Cauliflower rice, which is basically ground cauliflower in a food processor, is usually used as the go-to rice replacement, but who says that you have to eat cauliflower for every meal? Almost any vegetable that can be spiralized can be turned into rice. Simply make the noodles and then pulse them quickly in your food processor for a veggie rice. Turnips, carrots, squash, are also great rice substitutes.

Soups

Once you master the art of making noodles, you will see how they can easily be used for making delicious and nutritious wsoups. Instead of rice, egg, or wheat noodles, why not add veggie noodles to your soups and stews and boost the nutrients intake even more?

Omelets

Want to pack your morning omelets with tasty veggies? Why waste time chopping when you can easily spiralizer and incorporate them into your omelet the easiest and most hassle-free way? Any veggie that can be spiralized can be a great addition to your egg breakfasts.

Pizza and Sandwiches

Again, you can skip the whole chopping prep time by easily spiralizing your veggies that will not only save you time, but will also give your pizzas, wraps, and sandwiches a elegant look that will fancy up your dinner table.

Desserts

That's right, you can use pumpkin, squash, sweet potato, and zucchini noodles for making some amazingly delicious recipes, as you will see for yourself in the final chapter of this book.

THE BLADES

The blades used for spiralizing, obviously, depend on the type of spiralizer you have, however, since most spiralizers have these main three blades, I will briefly explain what they are best used for and which veggies go perfect with which blade.

Blade A

This is what we call the 'straight' blade that has no triangular blades, and makes long, flat, and ribbon like noodles. It is something similar to the noodles that can be made with a vegetable peeler. If you spiralizer potatoes with this noodle, you will make slices.

Best vegetables to use with this blades are potatoes, cucumbers, and zucchinis.

This blade is best for potato chips, or for noodles that are about to be served with a thicker sauce.

Blade B

This blade has large triangular blades, and make spaghetti-like noodles, mostly solid bucattini. Again, this blade is perfect for potatoes, zucchini, and cucumbers.

The most suggested use for this blade is when trying to make half-moons, whether for mac and cheese or slaw.

Blade C

The third blade had small triangular blades, and it is the blade that is used the most. This blade makes spaghetti or angel hair noodles, and it is the perfect choice for any vegetable that can be spiralized.

THE VEGETABLES

No, you cannot actually spiralizer sausage. Trust me, whatever comes to your mind has already been tested. It is true that the spiralizer is super versatile, however, there are a couple of rules that determine whether a veggie or fruit can actually be spiralized:

- The vegetables cannot be seeded, hollow, or have a really touch core.

- For best results, the vegetable has to at least have a diameter of 1.5 inches.

- For best results, the vegetable has to be at least 2 inches long.

- To be spiralizeable, the vegetable has to have a solid and firm flash. Juicy and squishy vegetables or fruits (such as tomato) cannot be spiralized.

Zucchini

Soft, easy to spiralizer and neutral in flavor, the zucchini is the most spiralized vegetable ever. It is perfect for many different dishes, and the perfect choice for making veggie pasta. You can even leave the peel on for extra nutrients.

Cucumber

Usually used with the straight or Blade A, you can have a beautifully displayed cucumber ribbons for your salads, in just seconds. Not recommended for pastas or rice, but the spiralized cucumber surely is the king of salads.

Bell Pepper

What better way to spice up your tacos that adding some spiralized bell pepper to it? If you want to slice an entire blade, use the straight blade for quick and easy spiralized slices. Just remove the seeds and pit when you finish, and that's it.

Parsnip

So similar to actual spaghetti, you can pretty much fool anyone with your parsnip noodles. Except your body of course. It will benefit the most. Blade B and C both work great with parsnips. Turnips are also great for spiralizing.

Carrot

Your salads and stir fries have never been easier to make. With the spiralizer you can have a bunch of spiralized carrots in seconds. Forget grating or peeling, and use the blades B and C for transforming this veggie into lovely fine noodles.

Sweet Potato

Anyone in the mood for some curly fries? Peel before spiralizing, and you will create beautiful potato noodles in no time. They can be used for variety of dishes, and work great with all of the blades.

Red Onion

There is no more crying with the spiralizer. If you have sensitive eyes than you know how challenging can chopping onions be. With the spiralizer, you can spiralizer an entire large onion in seconds, and with dry eyes. A perfect addition to stir-fries, salads, sauces, omelets, and pretty much all savory meals.

Cabbage

Whether red or green, slicing cabbage for a coleslaw can be super time consuming. But not with the spiralizer. With this appliance you can easily prep your coleslaws in mere seconds.

Beet

Maybe you still need gloves to avoid straining your fingers, but spiralizing instead of grating or slicing is way more convenient. These beautiful red or golden beets in seconds, can be the vibrant addition to any meal.

Fruits

The spiralizer is not only meant for making vegetable noodles. Some fruits can also be spiralized into long and beautiful ribbons. Plantains, apples, and pears, are the best choices for the spiralizer. You can give your salads a crunchy and sweet taste with some apple or pair noodles, or you can use these fruit noodles for your **crumbles, tarts, or other desserts.**

SPIRALIZING TIPS

The spiralizer is a super useful appliance that will create veggie noodles in mere seconds, without any hassle. However, you need to know a few things before embarking this spiralizer journey, to make sure that you will get the best results:

- Before you start, it is important to thoroughly wash the veggies you are about to spiralizer to avoid contamination. Use a brush when washing and wash the blades well.

- Trim the ends of the veggies before placing on the spiralizer to give a stable and flat base.

- Peel the root vegetables or the ones that have a tough core, to make it easier to cut and prevent your blades from damaging.

- If using long or wide vegetables, cut them in halves or in thirds to fit the frame.

- If the vegetables you are using and super hard and cannot be easily cut, you may want to try microwaving them for a minute or two before spiralizing.

- For narrow and firm vegetables, you will need to add some extra pressure when spiralizing.

- Snip the noodles to get the desired size.

- With the ribbon slices you can either get long ribbons or slices. This depends on the texture of the vegetables.

BREAKFAST RECIPES

Zucchini Pancakes

Serves: 1 \ Ready in: 30 minutes

Nutritional Info:

Calories 139, Carbohydrates 4 g, Fat 20 g, Protein 5 g

Ingredients:

½ cup skim Milk (preferably Almond)

1 tsp Vanilla Extract

1 cup pre-made Pancake Mix

1 tsp Cinnamon

½ tsp Nutmeg

1 small Zucchini (spiralized with the shredding blade)

1 tbsp Coconut Oil, melted

1 Egg

Maple Syrup, for serving

Directions:

1. Combine the pancake mix with the nutmeg and cinnamon in a bowl.
2. In another bowl, combine all of the wet ingredients.
3. Gradually pour the wet mixture into the bowl with the dry ingredients, whisking to combine.
4. Stir in the zucchini noodles.
5. Heat a skillet over medium heat and spray with cooking spray.
6. Add ⅓ of the mixture and cook for a few minutes on both sides, until set.
7. Repeat with the rest of the batter. Serve with maple syrup and enjoy.

Sweet Potato, Beans, and Spinach Tostadas

Serves: 4 \ Ready in: 40 minutes

Nutritional Info:

Calories 226, Carbohydrates 12 g, Fat 17 g, Protein 8 g

Ingredients:

5 Eggs

2 tbsp Olive Oil

1 Avocado, pitted, peeled, and sliced

1 Large Sweet Potato, spiralized with the shredding blade

¼ tsp Chili Powder

¼ tsp Garlic Powder

⅓ cup Salsa

1 cup Spinach, packed

1 cup refried Beans

chopped Cilantro, for garnishing

Directions:

1. Heat 1 tbsp olive oil in a skillet over medium heat. Add the potato noodles, season with chili and garlic powder, and cook for about 7 minutes.

2. Place the potatoes in a bowl and refrigerate for 5 minutes. Crack an egg into the bowl with the potatoes and toss them to combine. Heat the other tablespoon of oil in the same skillet over medium heat.

3. Add ¼ of the potato mixture in the skillet, flatten with a spatula and cook for about 3 minutes per side. Repeat with the rest of the potatoes. Divide the potato tostadas between 4 plates.

4. Spray the skillet with cooking spray and cook the remaining 4 eggs, until the whites become set.

5. Top the tostadas with spinach, beans, avocado, and a fried egg on top.

Sausage, Potato, and Pea Frittata

Serves: 4 \ Ready in: 30 minutes

Nutritional Info:

Calories 283, Carbohydrates 13 g, Fat 17 g, Protein 21 g

Ingredients:

8 Eggs, beaten

½ tsp Garlic Powder

½ cup Frozen Peas

1 Potato, spiralized with the shredding blade

2 Breakfast Sausages, sliced

1 tbsp Olive Oil

Salt and Pepper, to taste

Directions:

1. Preheat your oven to 425 degrees F.
2. Heat the olive oil in a skillet over medium heat.
3. Add the potato noodles, garlic powder, salt and pepper, and cook until set, about 10 minutes. Set aside.
4. Add the sausage and cook until brown, for about 5 minutes.
5. Stir in the potatoes and the peas.
6. Pour the eggs over and cook for 2 minutes.
7. Transfer the skillet to the oven and bake for 10 minutes.

Apple and Cranberry Oatmeal

Serves: 3 \ Ready in: 5 minutes

Nutritional Info:

Calories 322, Carbohydrates 50 g, Fat 11 g, Protein 11 g

Ingredients:

3 packages Instant Oats

1 Apple, spiralized with the angel hair blade

4 tbsp dried Cranberries

1 ounce crumbled Goat Cheese

3 tbsp chopped Walnuts

¾ cup Almond Milk

Directions:

1. Place each of the oat packages in a bowl and top with ⅔ cup of boiling water.
2. Stir until the oats absorb the liquid and become fluffed up.
3. Divide the rest of the ingredients between the bowls. Stir well to combine.

Zucchini, Tomato, and Mozzarella Egg Muffins

Serves: 6 (12 muffins) \ Ready in: 40 minutes

Nutritional Info:

Calories 278, Carbohydrates 8 g, Fat 6 g, Protein 22 g

Ingredients:

1 large Zucchini, spiralized with the shredding blade

18 Eggs, beaten

3 cups quartered Cherry Tomatoes

½ cup Basil

¾ cup shredded Mozzarella

Salt and Pepper, to taste

Directions:

1. Preheat your oven to 375 degrees F.
2. Spray your muffin tins with cooking spray. Fill the tins halfway with zucchini noodles.
3. Add the basil and tomatoes on top and season with salt and black pepper.
4. Top with mozzarella cheese.
5. Pour the eggs over, filling the tins ¾ to the top.
6. Place in the oven and bake for 25 minutes.

Scrambled Eggs with Beet and Feta

Serves: 1 \ Ready in: 15 minutes

Nutritional Info:

Calories 433, Carbohydrates 10 g, Fat 33 g, Protein 24 g

Ingredients:

3 Eggs, beaten

3 tbsp crumbled Feta Cheese

½ tbsp Olive Oil

1 small Beetroot, spiralized with the angel hair blade

¼ Avocado, cubed

Salt and Black Pepper, to taste

Directions:

1. Heat the olive oil in a skillet over medium heat.
2. Add the beet noodles and cook for about 5 minutes.

3. Stir in the eggs, avocado, and season with salt and pepper.
4. Stir while cooking until the eggs are set. Stir in the feta cheese.

Red Potato Waffles with Chorizo

Serves: 2 \ Ready in: 35 minutes

Nutritional Info:

Calories 244, Carbohydrates 15 g, Fat 15 g, Protein 13 g

Ingredients:

1 Large Red Potato, spiralized (preferably with the angel hair blade)

1 tsp chopped Parsley

2 ¼ ounces Chorizo, crumbled

¼ tsp Paprika

1 Egg

¼ tsp Garlic Powder

Salt and Pepper, to taste

Directions:

1. Preheat your waffle iron. Heat a skillet over medium heat.
2. Add the chorizo and cook for about 7 minutes. Set aside in a bowl.
3. Add the potato noodles to the skillet along with the seasonings.
4. Cover the skillet and cook for about 5 minutes or until the potato noodles become wilted.
5. Transfer to the bowl with chorizo.
6. Add the egg and parsley and mix to incorporate the ingredients well.
7. Spray the waffle iron and pack the chorizo/potato mixture in it.
8. Cook the waffles for about 7 minutes.

Breakfast Bowl the Mexican Way

Serves: 4 \ Ready in: 30 minutes

Nutritional Info:

Calories 375, Carbohydrates 30 g, Fat 7 g, Protein 18 g

Ingredients:

2 tbsp chopped Cilantro

½ tsp Garlic Powder

1 Avocado, mashed

8 Eggs, beaten

¾ cup chopped Tomatoes

1 tbsp Olive Oil

¼ tsp Paprika

½ cup Black Beans

1 Large Potato, spiralized as desired

¼ cup chopped Onion

1 tsp minced Jalapeno

¼ tsp Chili Powder

Juice of ½ Lime

Directions:

1. Heat the olive oil in a skillet over medium heat. Add the potato noodles, chili powder, paprika, and garlic powder. Cover the skillet and cook for 7 minutes.
2. Meanwhile, combine the beans, avocado, onion, jalapeno, lime juice, and cilantro in a bowl.
3. Transfer the potato noodles to a bowl. Spray the skillet with cooking spray.
4. Add the eggs in the skillet, scramble, and cook for a couple of minutes until set.
5. Place the eggs on top of the potato noodles, and top with the avocado/beans mixture.

Bell Pepper Omelet with Onions and Tomatoes

Serves: 1 \ Ready in: 20 minutes

Nutritional Info:

Calories 327, Carbohydrates 22 g, Fat 20 g, Protein 16 g

Ingredients:

1 tsp Olive Oil

1 Bell Pepper, spiralized

½ small Onion, spiralized

⅓ cup diced Tomatoes

¼ Avocado, sliced

¼ tsp Thyme

2 Eggs, beaten

Salt and Pepper, to taste

Directions:

1. Heat the olive oil in a skillet over medium heat.
2. Add the spiralzied onions and bell peppers and cook for about 7 minutes.
3. Season with salt and pepper, and add the thyme.
4. Pour the beaten eggs over and sprinkle the tomatoes on top.
5. After 2 minutes, flip the omelet over and cook for 2 more minutes on the other side.
6. Serve the omelet topped with avocado slices.

Eggs in Sweet Potato Nests

Serves: 2 \ Ready in: 15 minutes

Nutritional Info:

Calories 221.3, Carbohydrates 17.2 g, Fat 13.6 g, Protein 7.7 g

Ingredients:

1 Sweet Potato, spiralized

1 tsp Garlic Powder

2 Eggs

1 ½ tbsp Butter, melted

Directions:

1. Melt 1 tbsp butter in a skillet over medium heat.
2. Add the potatoes, garlic powder and cook for 7 minutes. Transfer to a bowl.
3. Melt half of the remaining butter in the same skillet.
4. Add half of the cooked potatoes and make a hole in the middle.
5. Crack an egg in the hole and cook until the egg is set.
6. Repeat the process one more time.

Banana Pancakes with Cinnamon Apples

Serves: 12 \ Ready in: 15 minutes

Nutritional Info:

Calories 218, Carbohydrates 26 g, Fat 10 g, Protein 9 g

Ingredients:

4 Eggs, beaten

¼ tsp Cinnamon

2 Bananas

2 tsp Coconut Oil

1 Apple, spiralized (preferable with the angel hair blade)

Maple Syrup, for serving

Directions:

1. Mash the bananas in a bowl.
2. Add the eggs and mix to incorporate well.
3. Heat a skillet over medium heat and spray it with cooking spray.
4. Place half of the banana mixture in the skillet and cook for about 2 minutes per side.
5. Repeat the process with the remaining pancake. Set aside.
6. Melt the coconut oil in the same skillet.
7. Add the spiralized apples and sprinkle them with cinnamon.
8. Cook the apples for about 3 minutes, or until wilted.
9. Serve the pancakes topped with the apples and drizzled with maple syrup.

Potato Bagels

Serves: 3 \ Ready in: 35 minutes

Nutritional Info:

Calories 212, Carbohydrates 28 g, Fat 8 g, Protein 8 g

Ingredients:

2 Russet Potatoes, spiralized

2 Eggs, beaten

1 tbsp Olive Oil

1 tsp Poppy Seeds

1 tsp Onion Powder

¼ tsp Pepper

½ tsp Salt

1 tsp Sesame Seeds

1 tsp Garlic Powder

Directions:

1. Preheat your oven to 400 degrees and spray a donut pan with cooking spray.
2. Heat the olive oil in a skillet over medium heat.
3. Add the potato noodles and cook for about 10 minutes.
4. Transfer to a bowl.
5. Add the eggs in the bowl and mix to combine.
6. Pour the mixture into the donut pan.
7. Place in the oven and bake for 15 minutes.
8. In a small bowl, combine all of the remaining ingredients.
9. Top the bagels with that mixture.

Breakfast Hash with Kale

Serves: 2 \ Ready in: 25 minutes

Nutritional Info:

Calories 369, Carbohydrates 14.2 g, Fat 31.7 g, Protein 8.8 g

Ingredients:

4 Kale Leaves, chopped

1 Medium Sweet Potato, spiralized

1 Red Bell Pepper, spiralized

¼ tsp Cumin

⅛ tsp Salt

¼ tsp Cumin

½ Onion, spiralized

⅛ tsp Black Pepper

2 Eggs

¼ cup Olive Oil

Directions:

1. Heat about 3/4 of the olive oil in a skillet over medium heat.
2. Add the bell peppers, onion, potatoes, paprika, cumin, salt, and pepper.
3. Cook for about 15 minutes, stirring occasionally.
4. Stir chopped kale in the las 4 minutes of cooking.
5. In another bowl, heat the remaining olive oil.
6. Crack the eggs into it and cook until set.
7. Divide the hash brown mixture between two plates and top with a fried egg.

SALAD RECIPES

Beet and Hummus Salad with Arugula

Serves: 4 \ Ready in: 20 minutes

Nutritional Info:

Calories 154, Carbohydrates 11 g, Fat 11 g, Protein 5 g

Ingredients:

6 cups Baby Arugula

10 ounces Hummus

1 Beet, spiralized

3 tbsp Olive Oil

½ tsp Dijon Mustard

¼ cup chopped Walnuts

2 tbsp Lemon Juice

Salt and Pepper, to taste

Directions:

1. Whisk together the lemon juice, mustard, and olive oil, along with salt and pepper.
2. Combine the rest of the ingredients in a large bowl.
3. Our the dressing over and mix to coat well.
4. Serve and enjoy!

Kale and Sweet Potato Salad with Chickpeas and Cashews

Serves: 4 \ Ready in: 55 minutes

Nutritional Info:

Calories 317, Carbohydrates 43 g, Fat 12 g, Protein 13 g

Ingredients:

1 ½ tbsp Olive Oil, divided

1 large Sweet Potato, spiralized

¼ tsp Garlic Powder

3 cups chopped Kale, packed

15 ounces canned Chickpeas, rinsed, drained, and patted dry

1 tsp Chili Powder

¼ tsp Cayenne Pepper

½ tsp Cumin

¼ cup Cashews

½ tsp Mustard

½ tbsp Lemon Juice

¼ cup Almond Milk

1 Garlic Clove, minced

Salt and Pepper, to taste

Directions:

1. Preheat your oven to 400 degrees F.
2. Place chickpeas, cumin, cayenne pepper, chilli powder, ½ tbsp olive oil and salt. Mix to coat the chickpeas well.
3. Arrange them in a single layer on a lined baking sheet and bake for 30 minutes.
4. Heat the remaining olive oil in a skillet over medium heat.

5. Add the potato noodles, garlic powder, and salt and pepper, and cook for about 7 minutes. Set aside.

6. Place the cashews, almond milk, garlic, mustard, lemon juice, and salt and pepper, in a food processor, and process until smooth.

7. Place the kale in the skillet where the potatoes were cooked and sauté for 3 minutes, or until wilted.

8. Combine the kale, potato noodles, and chickpeas in a large serving bowl.

9. Pour the dressing over and serve.

Shrimp Cucumber Salad

Serves: 4 \ Ready in: 25 minutes

Nutritional Info:

Calories 278, Carbohydrates 8 g, Fat 18 g, Protein 35 g

Ingredients:

1 pound medium Shrimp, deveined

1 Avocado, sliced

e Cucumber, spiralized

chopped Romaine Salad

Olive Oil

arlic Powder

Dressing:

½ cup Yogurt

1 tbsp Olive Oil

1 Garlic Clove, pressed

3 tbsp Lemon Juice

¼ tsp Salt

¼ cup grated Parmesan Cheese

2 tsp Worcestershire Sauce

1 tsp Dijon Mustard

Pinch of Black Pepper

Directions:

1. Whisk together all of the dressing ingredients in a large bowl.
2. Heat a skillet over medium heat.
3. Add the shrimp, oil, and garlic powder, and stir to combine.
4. Cook the shrimp for about 2-3 minutes on each side.
5. Place the shrimp, cucumber, and romaine lettuce in the bowl with the dressing.
6. Toss to coat the salad well.

Simple Carrot Salad

Serves: 6 \ Ready in: 10 minutes

Nutritional Info:

Calories 54, Carbohydrates 8 g, Fat 2 g, Protein 1 g

Ingredients:

4 Large Carrots

2 tbsp Orange Juice

2 tbsp Vinegar

1 tbsp Tamari Sauce

1 tsp Honey

3 Scallions, sliced

2 tbsp toasted Sesame Seeds

1 tsp toasted Sesame Oil (Olive Oil works fine too)

¼ tsp Garlic Powder

Directions:

1. Spiralize the carrots into long and thin strips.
2. Whisk the orange juice, honey, tamari, oil, vinegar, and garlic powder, in a bowl.
3. Add the carrots and scallions to the bowl, and toss to coat them well.
4. Sprinkle the sesame seeds over.

Veggie Quinoa Salad

Serves: 6 \ Ready in: 25 minutes plus 1 hour chilling

Nutritional Info:

Calories 333, Carbohydrates 45 g, Fat 15 g, Protein 9 g

Ingredients:

1 cup chopped Dill

1 Cucumber, spiralized

1 cup fresh Parsley

2 tsp Sea Salt

1 Bell Pepper, spiralized

2 cups Quinoa, rinsed and drained

½ cup Lemon Juice

¼ cup Olive Oil

½ Red Onion, spiralized

10 Olives, chopped

4 cups Water

1 cup minced Green Onions

¼ tsp Black Pepper

Directions:

1. Combine the water and quinoa in a pot over medium heat, and bring the mixture to a boil.
2. Lower the heat and cook covered until the water is absorbed, about 15 minutes.
3. Fluff the quinoa with a fork and set aside to cool.
4. Place the lemon juice, black pepper, sea salt, and olive oil, in a large bowl.
5. Whisk to combine.
6. Add the quinoa and toss to coat well. Stir in the remaining ingredients.
7. Let the salad sit in the fridge for about 1 hour before serving.

Creamy Chicken, Carrot, and Zucchini Salad

Serves: 4 \ Ready in: 30 minutes

Nutritional Info:

Calories 242, Carbohydrates 12 g, Fat 3 g, Protein 38 g

Ingredients:

2 Skinless and Boneless Chicken Breasts

1 tbsp Apple Cider Vinegar

¼ tsp Garlic Powder

5 tbsp Hot Sauce

6 ounces Greek Yogurt

2 Large Zucchini, spiralized

1 Large Carrot, spiralized

¼ cup crumbled Blue Cheese

½ cup halved Cherry Tomatoes

¼ cup canned Corn

Directions:

1. Pace the chicken in a pot and cover with water. Place over high heat and bring it to a boil. Reduce the heat to medium, and cook for 12 minutes, or until no longer pink.

2. Meanwhile whisk together the vinegar, yogurt, hot sauce, and garlic powder in a large bowl

3. Shred the chicken with two forks and add it to the bowl, along with the rest of the ingredients. Stir to combine.

Bell Pepper and Artichoke Antipasto

Serves: 4 \ Ready in: 40 minutes

Nutritional Info:

Calories 107, Carbohydrates 9 g, Fat 6 g, Protein 5 g

Ingredients:

2 Bell Peppers (preferably in different colors), spiralized

1 ¼ tsp dried Oregano

1 ½ cups canned Artichoke Hearts, quartered

1 tsp Olive Oil

¼ cup cubed Provolone Cheese

½ cup halved Olives

2 cups mixed Greens

1 tbsp chopped Basil

Salt and Pepper, to taste

Directions:

1. Preheat your oven to 450 degrees F and line two baking sheets with waxed paper.

2. Place the bell peppers on one sheet and sprinkle with half the oregano and salt and pepper.

3. Arrange the artichokes on the other sheet, drizzle with the olive oil and sprinkle with the rest of the oregano, as well as salt and pepper.

4. Bake them for 20 minutes.

5. Place the roasted peppers and artichokes in a large bowl and stir in the rest of the ingredients.

Golden Beet Salad with Arugula and Figs

Serves: 2 \ Ready in: 30 minutes

Nutritional Info:

Calories 262, Carbohydrates 26 g, Fat 17 g, Protein 4 g

Ingredients:

3 cups Arugula, packed

1 large Golden Beet, spiralized

4 Figs, quartered

2 tbsp Olive Oil

½ tsp Dijon Mustard

1 tsp Honey

1 tbsp Sunflower Seeds

1 tsp Lemon Juice

1 tbsp Red Wine Vinegar

Salt and Pepper, to taste

1. Directions:

2. Whisk together the honey, lemon juice, olive oil, vinegar, mustard, and salt and pepper, in a small bowl.

3. In another bowl, combine all of the remaining ingredients.

4. Pour the dressing over and toss to coat well.

5. Refrigerate for 10 minutes before serving.

Tuna Salad with Apples, Chard, and Pecans

Serves: 1 \ Ready in: 10 minutes

Nutritional Info:

Calories 262, Carbohydrates 16, Fat 13 g, Protein 21 g

Ingredients:

6 Chard Leaves, chopped

1 Large Apple, spiralized

1 tbsp Apple Cider Vinegar

15 ounces canned Tina

1 tsp Honey

2 tsp Lemon Juice

¼ cup chopped Pecans

1 tsp Dijon Mustard

½ tbsp Olive Oil

1 tbsp Water

Salt and Pepper, to taste

Directions:

1. Whisk together the honey, oil, vinegar, water, lemon juice, mustard, and salt and pepper, in a small bowl.
2. Place the chard, apples, and pecans in a serving bowl.
3. Pour the dressing over and toss to combine.
4. Place the tuna on top.

Lemony Kohlrabi and Radish Salad

Serves: 1 \ Ready in: 15 minutes plus 30 minutes chilling

Nutritional Info:

Calories 68, Carbohydrates 7 g, Fat 5 g, Protein 1 g

Ingredients:

1 Large Kohlrabi, spiralized

2 large Radishes, spiralized

3 Asparagus Spears, shaved (with a veggie peeler)

2 tbsp Apple Cider Vinegar

juice of half Lemon

1 tbsp Olive Oil

1 tbsp chopped Chives

1 tbsp roasted Sunflower Seeds

Salt and Pepper, to taste

Directions:

1. Place the honey, olive oil, lemon, chives, vinegar, and salt and pepper in a large bowl.
2. Whisk to combine.
3. Place the kohlrabi, radishes, and asparagus in the bowl with the dressing.
4. Toss to coat well.
5. Top with roasted sunflower seeds.
6. Let sit for about 30 minutes in the fridge before serving.

Chicken and Apple Salad Cups with Grapes and Walnuts

Serves: 4 \ Ready in: 30 minutes

Nutritional Info:

Calories 212, Carbohydrates 13 g, Fat 11 g, Protein 17 g

Ingredients:

1 Large Chicken Breast

½ cup Walnuts

4 Lettuce Leaves

1 Celery Stalk, diced

1 large Gala Apple, spiralized

1 cup Grapes, halved

⅔ cup plus 2 tbsp Greek Yogurt

1 tbsp Lemon Juice

½ tsp Garlic Powder

1 tbsp Dijon Mustard

Salt and Pepper, to taste

Directions:

1. Place the chicken in a pot and cover it with water. Place over high heat and bring to a boil. Reduce the heat to medium and cook for about 12 minutes, or until cooked through.
2. Shred the chicken with two forks. Heat a skillet over medium heat and add the walnuts.
3. Toast them for about 5 minutes, or until darkened and fragrant.
4. Whisk together the yogurt, mustard, lemon juice, and garlic powder, along with salt and pepper, in a large bowl.
5. Add apples, grapes, walnuts, chicken, and celery. Toss to combine well. Divide the salad between 4 lettuce cups.

Prosciutto and Mozzarella Cantaloupe Salad

Serves: 4 \ Ready in: 20 minutes

Nutritional Info:

Calories 215, Carbohydrates 10 g, Fat 15 g, Protein 12 g

Ingredients:

2 tbsp Olive Oil

6 Mozzarella Balls, quartered

4 ounces Prosciutto, cut into strips

1 medium Cantaloupe, spiralized

1 tbsp Lime Juice

1 tbsp chopped Mint

1 tsp Honey

Directions:

1. Whisk together the honey, olive oil, lime juice, and mint, in a large bowl.
2. Place the cantaloupe and mozzarella in the bowl with the dressing and toss to coat well. Arrange the salad on a serving bowl. Add the prosciutto strips.

Squash Salad with Minty Dressing

Serves: 2 \ Ready in: 15 minutes

Nutritional Info:

Calories 97, Carbohydrates 12 g, Fat 6 g, Protein 3 g

Ingredients:

3 Summer Squash, spiralized

1 tbsp chopped Basil

1 tsp chopped Mint

1 large Celery Stalk, sliced

¼ tsp Cumin

½ tsp Lemon Zest

2 tsp Lemon Juice

2 tsp Olive Oil

Pinch of Red Pepper Flakes

Salt and Pepper, to taste

Directions:

1. Place all of the ingredients in a large bowl. Season with salt and pepper.
2. Toss to combine well. Serve and enjoy!

Sweet and Savory Pear Salad

Serves: 1 \ Ready in: 15 minutes

Nutritional Info:

Calories 413, Carbohydrates 37.7 g, Fat 21.6 g, Protein 9.2 g

Ingredients:

1 Red Anjou Pear, spiralized

⅛ cup chopped Pecans

¼ cup Fresh Blueberries

1 tbsp crumbled Goat Cheese

1 tbsp favorite salad dressing

Directions:

1. Place the pear noodles and dressing in a bowl. Toss to coat well.
2. Add the pecans, blueberries, and goat cheese. Toss to combine.

SOUPS AND STEWS

Carrot Noodle Chicken Soup with Leeks

Serves: 4 \ Ready in: 35 minutes

Nutritional Info:

Calories 173, Carbohydrates 7 g, Fat 10 g, Protein 11 g

Ingredients:

2 tbsp Olive Oil

2 Large Carrots, spiralized

6 cups Chicken Broth

1 ½ cups cooked and shredded Chicken

3 Garlic Cloves, minced

2 Leeks, sliced

2 Celery Stalks, diced

1 Bay Leaf

¼ cup Parsley

4 Thyme Sprigs

1 tbsp chopped Rosemary

Salt and Pepper, to taste

Directions:

1. Heat the oil in a large pot over medium heat. Add leeks, celery, and garlic, and cook for about 5 minutes.

2. Add 1 cup of water, chicken broth, bay leaf, thyme, and rosemary, and bring the mixture to a boil. Reduce the heat to low, add the chicken and carrots, and cook for about 9 minutes.

3. Discard the bay leaf. Top with parsley and serve.

Chard and White Bean Soup

Serves: 4 \ Ready in: 30 minutes

Nutritional Info:

Calories 188, Carbohydrates 30 g, Fat 5 g, Protein 9 g

Ingredients:

6 cups chopped Chard

1 tbsp Olive Oil

6 cups Veggie Broth

2 Celery Stalks, diced

2 Carrots, spiralized

1 Celery Root, spiralized

14 ½ ounces canned White Beans, drained and rinsed

2 Garlic Cloves, minced

¾ cup White Onion, finely chopped

2 tbsp chopped Thyme

¼ tsp Red Pepper Flakes

4 tbsp grated Parmesan Cheese, for garnishing

Directions:

1. Heat the olive oil in a large pot over medium heat.
2. Add onions and celery, and cook for 5 minutes.
3. Add garlic and cook for 30 more seconds, just until fragrant.
4. Pour in the veggie broth and along with the red pepper flakes and thyme
5. Bring the mixture to a boil.
6. Reduce the heat, and celery and carrot noodles, chard, and beans.
7. Cook for about 7 minutes (or more if you like your noodles super tender).
8. Serve the soup topped with a tbsp of parmesan cheese, if you want to.

Lamb Stew with Squash

Serves: 6 \ Ready in: 2 hours and 55 minutes

Nutritional Info:

Calories 290, Carbohydrates 17.3 g, Fat 17.1 g, Protein 18 g

Ingredients:

1 Onion, chopped

2 tbsp Vegetable Oil, divided

1 ½ pounds Lamb, cut into cubes

2 garlic Cloves, minced

2 Thyme Sprigs

1 Rosemary Sprig

2 ½ cups spiralized Squash

28 ounces canned chopped Tomatoes

2 cups Beef Broth

¾ cups sliced or spiralized Carrots

Directions:

1. Preheat your oven to 325 degrees F.
2. Heat half of the oil in a Dutch oven over medium heat.
3. Add the lamb and cook until browned on all sides, 5-10 minutes. Set aside.
4. Heat the remaining oil and add onion, carrots (if using sliced), and garlic.
5. Cook for 3-5 minutes.
6. Stir in tomatoes, lamb, thyme, rosemary, and beef broth. Bring the mixture to a boil.
7. Cover the Dutch oven and place in the oven. Cook for 2 hours.
8. Stir in the squash noodles and carrot (if using spiralized), return to oven, and cook for additional 25 minutes.

Lentils Soup

Serves: 6 \ Ready in: 55 minutes

Nutritional Info:

Calories 169, Carbohydrates 25 g, Fat 5 g, Protein 6 g

Ingredients:

2 tbsp Olive Oil

6 cups Veggie Broth

28 ounces canned Tomatoes, diced

2 Celery Stalks, diced

½ tsp Oregano

2 Carrots, spiralized

2 Turnips, spiralized

1 cup Lentils

2 Bay Leaves

2 tsp Lemon Juice

3 Garlci Cloves, minced

½ tsp Basil

½ Onion, finely chopped

Salt and Pepper, to taste

Directions:

1. Heat the olive oil in a pot over medium heat. Add onion and celery and cook for about 4 minutes. Add garlic and cook for additional 30 seconds.

2. Add tomatoes, veggie broth, basil, thyme, bay leaves, and season with salt and pepper.

3. Cover the pot and bring the mixture to a boil. Reduce the heat and let simmer for about 20 minutes.

4. Discard the bay leaves and add the carrot and turnip noodles and cook for about 7 more minutes. Stir in the lemon juice, serve, and enjoy!

Slow-Cooked Beef Bourignon

Serves: 6 \ Ready in: 5 hours and 35 minutes

Nutritional Info:

Calories 548, Carbohydrates 6 g, Fat 32 g, Protein 50 g

Ingredients:

5 Bacon Slices, cubed

3 Garlic Cloves, minced

1 pound Mushrooms, sliced

3 pounds Beef, cut into cubes

4 Thyme Sprigs

1 tbsp Tomato Paste

3 Celery Stalks, diced

1 Yellow Onion, spiralized

1 Large Carrot, spiralized

1 cup Beef Broth

1 cup Red Wine

Salt and Pepper, to taste

Directions:

1. Heat a skillet over medium heat. Add bacon cubes and cook until crispy. Set aside on a paper towel.

2. Season the beef with salt and pepper, and add to the skillet.

3. Cook for about 3 minutes on all sides, until browned. Transfer the meat and bacon in your slow cooker.

4. Stir in the rest of the ingredients, except the carrot noodles.

5. Cover the cooker and cook for 4 hours on High. Stir in the carrot noodles and cover partially.

6. Cook for another 1 hour. Discard the bay leaves and serve.

Pesto Soup with Zucchini and Chicken

Serves: 4 \ Ready in: 35 minutes

Nutritional Info:

Calories 290, Carbohydrates 12 g, Fat 5 g, Protein 21 g

Ingredients:

2 Zucchinis, spiralized

1 Carrot, spiralized

2 Celery Stalks, diced

6 cups Chicken Broth

2 Garlic Cloves, minced

2 cups shredded Leftover Chicken

½ Red Onion, finely chopped

1 tbsp Olive Oil

Pesto:

1 tbsp Olive Oil

1 Garlic Clove, minced

1 tbsp Pine Nuts

2 cups Basil, packed

2 tbsp grated Parmesan Cheese

Salt and Pepper, to taste

Directions:

1. Heat the olive oil in a large pot.
2. Add onions and celery, and cook until soft, about 5 minutes.
3. Add garlic and cook for 30 more seconds.
4. Pour in the broth and bring the mixture to a boil.
5. Add carrots and cook for 3 minutes.

6. Reduce the heat to low, add the zucchini noodles, and cook for 5 more minutes.

7. Meanwhile, place all of the pesto ingredients in a food processor, and process until smooth.

8. Stir the pesto into the soup.

Veggie Stew

Serves: 5 \ Ready in: 1 hour

Nutritional Info:

Calories 259, Carbohydrates 47 g, Fat 4 g, Protein 11 g

Ingredients:

3 cups chopped Kale

1 large Rutabaga, spiralized

1 cup Celery Noodles

1 cup Carrot Noodles

2 cups Veggie Broth

15 ounces canned diced Tomatoes

15 ounces canned Cannellini Beans, drained and rinsed

3 Garlic Cloves, minced

1 tbsp Olive Oil

½ cup diced Sweet Onion

½ tsp Red Pepper Flakes

1 tsp dried Thyme

1 tsp dried Oregano

1 Bay Leaf

¼ cup Red Wine

Salt and Pepper, to taste

Directions:

1. Preehat your oven to 425 degrees F.
2. Line a baking sheet with parchment paper and place the rutabaga noodles on it. Spray them with cooking spray and bake for 5 minutes.
3. Heat the olive oil in a large pot. Add onions, garlic, and red pepper flakes.
4. Cook for 5 minutes. Add beans, tomatoes, broth, red wine, kale, bay leaf, oregano, and thyme. Add salt and pepper, as well.
5. Bring the mixture to a boil, cover, reduce the heat and let cook for 20 minutes.
6. Stir in the carrot and celery noodles, and cook for 8 more minutes.
7. Stir in the bakes rutabaga noodles. Discard the bay leaf and serve.

Meatless Bean Chili with Zoodles

Serves: 6 \ Ready in: 1 hour

Nutritional Info:

Calories 303, Carbohydrates 55 g, Fat 5 g, Protein 17 g

Ingredients:

½ Red Onion, diced

1 tbsp Olive Oil

2 Bell Peppers, spiralized

2 Zucchinis, spiralized

2 Celery Stalks, diced

2 Garlic Cloves, minced

2 Carrots, sliced

1 Jalapeno Pepper, diced

14 ounces canned Pinto Beans, drained and rinsed

14 ounces Cannellini Beans, drained and rinsed

14 ounces canned diced Tomatoes

8 ounces Tomato Sauce

1 tbsp Chili Powder

Directions:

1. Heat the olive oil in a large pot. Add onion and cook for about 5 minutes, or until translucent.

2. Add carrot, celery, garlic, and jalapeno, and cook for 10 minutes.

3. Add the tomatoes, tomato sauce, cumin, oregano, chilli powder, and the beans. Bring the mixture to a boil, then lower the heat, and let simmer for 20 minutes.

4. Add the pepper noodles and cook for 8-10 more minutes. Add the zucchini noodles and let cook for 4 more minutes.

Italian Sausage Soup with Carrot Noodles and Kale

Serves: 4 \ Ready in: 35 minutes

Nutritional Info:

Calories 339, Carbohydrates 12 g, Fat 22 g, Protein 22 g

Ingredients:

¾ pound Italian Sausage

½ cup diced Onions

6 cups Chicken Broth

2 Carrots, spiralized

¼ cup Parmesan Cheese

4 cups Kale

1 tsp Oregano

2 Garlic Cloves, minced

1 tsp Red Pepper Flakes

Directions:

1. Heat a large pot over medium heat.
2. Add the sausage and cook it while crumbling it with a wooden spoon, about 15 minutes.
3. Add onions and garlic, and cook for 3 more minutes.
4. Add the ale and cook for 1 minute, until wilted.
5. Stir in oregano and broth, and bring the mixture to a boil.
6. Stir in the carrot noodles.
7. Cook for 7 minutes, or until they reach your preferred density.
8. Serve topped with parmesan cheese.

Quick Onion Soup with Mushrooms and Carrot Noodles

Serves: 4 \ Ready in: 20 minutes

Nutritional Info:

Calories 46, Carbohydrates 5 g, Fat 3 g, Protein 2 g

Ingredients:

1 Large Onion, diced

2 Celery Stalks, diced

6 cups Water

8 ounces White Button Mushrooms, sliced

1 Large Carrot, spiralized

2 Garlic Cloves, minced

2 tsp Olive Oil

3 Scallions, diced

¼ tsp White Pepper

Salt, to taste

Directions:

1. Heat the oil in a pot over medium heat.
2. Add the onions and cook for about 5 minutes.
3. Add water, garlic, celery, white pepper, and salt.
4. Bring the mixture to a boil. Reduce the heat and let simmer for 1 minute.
5. Strain the vegetables and reserve the liquid.
6. Bring the liquid back to a simmer, and add the mushrooms and carrots.
7. Cook for 5 minutes. Stir in the scallions and cook for one more minute.

Curried Broccoli and Carrot Soup

Serves: 4 \ Ready in: 45 minutes

Nutritional Info:

Calories 200, Carbohydrates 21 g, Fat 10.5 g, Protein 6 g

Ingredients:

1 tbsp Olive Oil

2 ½ cups Broccoli Florets

2 Carrots, spiralized

1 ¾ cups skim Milk

14 ounces canned Tomatoes

1 ½ cups Vegetable Soup

¼ tsp Cumin

1 tbsp Curry Powder

2 Garlic Cloves, minced

½ Onion, diced

2 tsp minced Ginger

1 Red Potato, spiralized

¼ tsp Red Pepper Flakes

Directions:

1. Heat the olive oil in a pot over medium heat.
2. Add onion and ginger and cook for 3 minutes. Ad garlic and cook until fragrant, about 30 seconds.
3. Stir in cumin, curry powder, red pepper flakes, and broccoli.
4. Add the tomatoes, milk, and broth, and bring the mixture to a boil.
5. Add the carrot and potato noodles and cook for about 7 minutes.

Turkey Chilli

Serves: 6 \ Ready in: 1 hour and 10 minutes

Nutritional Info:

Calories 506, Carbohydrates 24.1g, Fat 31.9 g, Protein 34.7 g

Ingredients:

1 ½ pound ground Turkey

1 tsp Coriander

2 tbsp Vegetable Oil, divided

1 tsp Oregano

2 tbsp Tomato Paste

14 ounces Beef Broth

7 ounces Salsa

1 tsp Chilli Flakes

1 Onion, diced

1 Bunch Green Onions, chopped

1 Green Bell Pepper, spiralized

3 Zucchini, spiralized

1 cup Cheddar Cheese, shredded

1 cup Sour Cream

7 ounces chopped Green Chilies

14 ounces canned crushed Tomatoes

Directions:

1. Heat 1 tbsp of the oil in a large pot over medium heat.
2. Add turkey and season it with oregano, coriander, chili flakes, and tomato paste.
3. Cook until the meat is browned.
4. Add beef broth, and cook for 5 minutes.
5. Stir in tomatoes, salsa, and chilies, and cook for 10 minutes.
6. In a skillet, heat 1 tbsp of the oil.
7. Add onion and cook for 5 minutes.
8. Stir the onions, along with the pepper noodles, into the chili.
9. After 7 minutes, add the zucchini noodles, and cook for 7 more minutes.
10. Stir in cheddar and sour cream.

Zoodle Chicken Soup

Serves: 6 \ Ready in: 45 minutes

Nutritional Info:

Calories 208, Carbohydrates 8.9g, Fat 9.5 g, Protein 21.6 g

Ingredients:

1 cup diced Celery

3 Garlic Cloves, minced

2 tbsp Olive Oil

1 cup sliced Carrots

¾ pound cooked Chicken, cut into cubes

3 Zucchinis, spiralized

5 14–ounce cans Chicken Broth

½ tsp dried Basil

1 pinch dried Thyme

½ tsp dried Oregano

1 cup died Onion

Salt and Pepper, to taste

Directions:

1. Heat the olive oil in a pot over medium heat.
2. Add celery, onion and garlic, and cook for 5 minutes.
3. Pour the broth into the pot.
4. Stir in chicken and carrots, along with oregano, thyme, and basil.
5. Season with salt and pepper.
6. Bring the mixture to a boil.
7. Reduce the heat and let simmer for 17 minutes.
8. Stir in the zoodles and cook for 5 more minutes.

SANDWICHES, WRAPS, AND PIZZAS

Olive and Basil Potato Pizza

Serves: 4 \ Ready in: 40 minutes

Nutritional Info:

Calories 198, Carbohydrates 17 g, Fat 11 g, Protein 10 g

Ingredients:

2 large Russet Potatoes, spiralized

3 Eggs, beaten

½ cup Marinara Sauce

12 Large Black Olives, pitted and sliced

A few Basil Leaves, chopped

1 tbsp Olive Oil

½ tsp Garlic Powder

5 ounces shredded Mozzarella Cheese

Directions:

1. Preheat your oven to 400 degrees F. Heat the olive oil in a skillet.
2. Add the potato noodles and season with garlic powder.
3. Cook until browned, about 10 minutes. Place in a bowl and add the eggs.
4. Combine the mixture well and return to the skillet.
5. Spread the potato and egg mixture, covering the bottom of the skillet completely. Bake for 12 minutes.
6. Sprinkle the mozzarella cheese over, and bake for another 5 minutes.
7. Place the marinara sauce in a pot and bring to a simmer.
8. Pour the sauce over the pizza, and top with basil and olives.

Cucumber and Turkey Sandwich with Hummus

Serves: 4 \ Ready in: 10 minutes

Nutritional Info:

Calories 197, Carbohydrates 23 g, Fat 6 g, Protein 14 g

Ingredients:

2 Whole Wheat Pittas, halved

1 Large English Cucumber, spiralized as desired

1 package of Applegate Rast Turkey deli slices (leftovers work fine too)

½ cup Hummus

Directions:

1. Divide the hummus between the 4 pita pockets.
2. Place the turkey slices into the pockets.Top with the cucumber noodles.

Cauliflower Burger with Apple & Cucumber

Serves: 2 \ Ready in: 2 hours and 10 minutes

Nutritional Info:

Calories 482, Carbohydrates 56 g, Fat 23 g, Protein 17 g

Ingredients:

2 tsp Onion Powder

¾ cup Almond Flour

½ cup Almond Milk

2 2 ½ -inches Cauliflower Steak Slices

½ cup Water

1 tsp Cumin

¼ tsp Salt

1 tsp Paprika

2 tsp Garlic Powder

1 tbsp Coconut Oil, melted

¼ tsp Pepper

½ cup Hot Sauce

2 Romaine Lettuce Leaves

2 Potato Buns

2 Tomato Slices

Slaw:

¼ cup Greek Yogurt

½ English Cucumber, spiralized

1 Granny Smith Apple, spiralized

2 tbsp Apple Cider Vinegar

2 tbsp Dijon Mustard

Salt and Pepper, to taste

Directions:

1. Preheat your oven to 450 degrees F. Line a cookie sheet with waxed paper.
2. Whisk together the milk, flour, water, and spices, in a bowl.
3. Dredge the cauliflower steaks in the mixture, making sure that they are coated well. Arrange on the cookie sheet and bake for 25 minutes. Combine the coconut oil and hot sauce.
4. Coat the cauliflower steaks with this mixture, then place them bacon on the baking sheet, and bake for additional 25 minutes.
5. Whisk together the slaw ingredients and combine them with the spiralized apple and cucumber. Cut the potato buns in half.
6. Assemble the burgers by placing a steak on one bun half and topping it with the slaw. Top with the other bun half.

Philly Cheese Sandwich on Mushrooms

Serves: 6 \ Ready in: 30 minutes

Nutritional Info:

Calories 172, Carbohydrates 7 g, Fat 14 g, Protein 9 g

Ingredients:

6 Large Portobello Mushroom Caps

2 tbsp Olive Oil

1 tsp Oregano

6 slices Provolone Cheese

½ tsp Garlic Powder

1 Onion, spiralized

2 Bell Peppers, spiralized

Directions:

1. Preheat your oven to 400 degrees F.
2. Line a cookie sheet with parchment paper.
3. Arrange the mushroom caps on the baking dish.
4. Spray with cooking spray.
5. Bake for about 10 minutes. Heat the olive oil in a skillet over medium heat.
6. Add the onion and pepper noodles.
7. Season with garlic powder and oregano.
8. Cook for about 10 minutes, or until caramelized.
9. Pack each of the portobello caps with the caramelized noodles.
10. Top with a slice of provolone cheese. Bake for 8 more minutes.

Bacon and Eggplant Pizza

Serves: 2 \ Ready in: 10 minutes

Nutritional Info:

Calories 339, Carbohydrates 19.5 g, Fat 18.8 g, Protein 24.5 g

Ingredients:

1 Eggplant, peeled and spiralized

1 tsp garlic Powder

1 tsp Oregano

⅓ cup Tomato Sauce

4 Mozzarella Slices

¼ cup shredded Mozzarella Cheese

4 Bacon Slices

1 tbsp Olive Oil

Directions:

1. Preheat your oven to 400 degrees F.
2. Heat the olive oil in a skillet over medium heat.
3. Add the eggplant and garlic powder and cook for about 10 minutes.
4. Spread the spiralized eggplant to cover the bottom of the skillet,
5. Arrange the mozzarella slices on top.
6. Top with the bacon slices.
7. Place in the oven and bake for 10 minutes.
8. Spread the tomato sauce over and sprinkle the shredded cheese on top.
9. Return to oven and bake for 5 more minutes.

Zucchini Grilled Sandwich

Serves: 4 \ Ready in: 10 minutes

Nutritional Info:

Calories 492, Carbohydrates 45.8 g, Fat 20.3 g, Protein 30.8 g

Ingredients:

4 cups Zucchini Noodles (s[iralized with the Angel Hair blade)

2 Large Eggs

2 slices Provolone Slices

½ cup Parmesan Cheese

¼ tsp Black Pepper

¾ cup All-Purpose Flour

Directions:

1. Preheat your oven to 450 degrees F and line a cookie sheet with parchment paper.
2. Place the zucchini in a bowl and let sit for about 30 minutes. Drain the excess water and return zucchini noodles to the bowl.
3. Add flour, eggs, pepper and parmesan cheese.
4. Mix well until combined,
5. Divide the zucchini into 4 patties and place on the baking sheet.
6. Bake for about 20 minutes, turning over once.
7. Place 1 cheese slice between 2 zucchini patties.
8. Heat a skillet over medium heat and spray with cooking spray.
9. Cook the grilled cheese sandwiches until the cheese is melted.

Peanut Butter and Jelly Sweet Potato Sandwich

Serves: 1 \ Ready in: 30 minutes

Nutritional Info:

Calories 470, Carbohydrates 51.5 g, Fat 21 g, Protein 11.1 g

Ingredients:

1 Sweet Potato, spiralized

1 ½ tbsp Peanut Butter

1 tbsp favorite Jelly

1 tbs Olive Oil

1 Large Egg White

Directions:

1. Heat half of the oil in a skillet over medium heat.
2. Add potato and cook for about 10 minutes.
3. Place in the fridge for 5 minutes.
4. Combine the potato with the egg white and make 2 patties out of the mixture.
5. Heat the remaining olive oil and cook the patties for about 2 minutes per side.
6. Spread the peanut butter on one pattie, and top it with the jelly.
7. Top the sandwich with the other pattie.

Pulled BBQ Carrot Sandwich

Serves: 4 \ Ready in: 1 hour

Nutritional Info:

Calories 224, Carbohydrates 40 g, Fat 5 g, Protein 4 g

Ingredients:

4 Buns

5 Large Carrots, spiralized

1 Red Onion, spiralized

½ tsp Olive Oil

Salt and Pepper, to taste

BBQ Sauce:

1 tsp salt

1 tbsp Lime Juice

3 Garlic Cloves

¼ cup Brown Sugar

1 cup Tomato Sauce

1 tsp Olive Oil

1 tbsp Cilantro

¼ tsp Cayenne Pepper

¼ tsp Cumin

¼ tsp White Pepper

1 tbsp Dark Molasses

¼ cup Apple Cider Vinegar

1 Pepper from a can of Peppers in Adobo Sauce, seeded

Directions:

1. Preheat your oven to 385 degrees F. Line a baking dish with waxed paper.
2. Place the carrot and onion noodles on the baking dish and drizzle with the olive oil. Cover the dish with aluminium foil and bake for 20 minutes.
3. Uncover and bake for additional 10 minutes. Meanwhile, place all of the sauce ingredients in a blender or food processor, and blend until smooth.
4. Transfer the sauce to a pan and place over medium heat. Bring to a boil, reduce the heat, and let simmer for 20 minutes.
5. Add the roasted noodles to the pan with sauce. Divide the noodles between the buns and serve.

Rich Veggie Wrap

Serves: 4 \ Ready in: 25 minutes

Nutritional Info:

Calories 284, Carbohydrates 36 g, Fat 12 g, Protein 10 g

Ingredients:

½ cup Hummus

4 Whole Grain Wraps

1 small Avocado. Sliced

1 large Carrot, spiralized

1 beet, spiralized

1 English Cucumber, spiralized

4 Pinches of Sprouts

2 cups Spinach

Directions:

1. On a flat surface, lay out one wrap.
2. Spread ¼ of the hummus, and top with ¼ of the remaining ingredients.

3. Wrap the wrap like you would wrap a burrito, and secure it with a toothpick.
4. Repeat the process with the rest of the ingredients.

Chicken Pita Sandwich with Veggie Noodles

Serves: 1 \ Ready in: 10 minutes

Nutritional Info:

Calories 327.7, Carbohydrates 25.8 g, Fat 14.9 g, Protein 24.2 g

Ingredients:

2 tsp Olive Oil

⅛ tsp Salt

½ tsp Garlic Powder

½ tsp Apple Cider Vinegar

3 ounces cooked and shredded Chicken

½ Large Whole Wheat Pita Bread

1 ounce spiralized Bell Pepper

¼ Cucumber, spiralized

¼ cup spiralized Onions

1 tbsp Sour Cream

1 tbsp chopped Basil

Directions:

1. Whisk together the oil, vinegar, salt, and basil, in a bowl.
2. Add cucumber, peppers, and onions to the bowl.
3. Toss to combine them well.
4. Spread the sour cream in the pocket o the pita bread.
5. Add the chicken in the pocket. Top with the seasoned noodles.

Zoodle Tacos

Serves: 2 \ Ready in: 30 minutes

Nutritional Info:

Calories 381, Carbohydrates 53 g, Fat 16 g, Protein 12 g

Ingredients:

1 Corn Ear

½ cup Black Beans

1 cup shredded Lettuce

1 tbsp minced Cilantro

1 Avocado, peeled

6 Taco Shells

½ cup Tomato Sauce

2 Zucchinis, spiralized

Salt and Pepper, to taste

Taco Seasoning:

1 tsp Cumin

½ tsp Chili Powder

¼ tsp Smoked Paprika

¼ tsp ground Coriander

⅛ tsp Oreano

⅛ tsp Garlic Powder

⅛ tsp Onion Powder

Salt and Pepper, to taste

Directions:

1. Place the corn in a pot with water and bring to a boil over medium heat.
2. Cook for about 2 minutes, or until you can easily pierce a fork through it.

3. Shave the kernels off the corn and set aside.
4. In a small bowl, combine the seasonings along with salt and pepper. Set aside.
5. Combine the tomato sauce and taco seasoning in a saucepan over medium heat. Simmer for about 5 minutes.
6. Meanwhile, mash the avocado along with the cilantro and salt and pepper.
7. Stir the corn zoodles, and beans, into the tomato sauce, and cook for 3 minutes.
8. Divide the zoodle mixture between the taco shells.
9. Top with the avocado mixture and lettuce.

SNACKS AND SIDE DISHES

Chili Shoestring Fries

Serves: 6 \ Ready in: 40 minutes

Nutritional Info:

Calories 155, Carbohydrates 29 g, Fat 4 g, Protein 4 g

Ingredients:

3 Large Potatoes, spiralized with the Angel Hair Blade

1 tsp Paprika

1 tsp Chili Powder

1 tsp Garlic Powder

1 ½ tbsp Olive Oil

Salt and Pepper, to taste

Directions:

1. Preheat your oven to 425 degrees F.
2. Line a baking sheet.
3. Place the potato noodles in a bowl, add the spices and drizzle the oil over.
4. Mix with your hands until coated well.
5. Arrange the potato noodles on the sheet, and bake for 25 minutes.
6. The fries should be cooked and crispy, however, since they can easily turn brown, check them after 20 minutes of cooking and take the brown parts out (if any).

Garlicky Potato and Gruyere Casserole

Serves: 6 \ Ready in: 1 hour and 15 minutes

Nutritional Info:

Calories 299, Carbohydrates 40 g, Fat 10 g, Protein 12 g

Ingredients:

1 tbsp Olive Oil

1 ½ tbsp Fresh Thyme Leaves, spiralized with the straight blade

3 pounds Yukon Gold Potatoes

3 Garlic Cloves, minces

3 tbsp grated Parmesan Cheese

1 ½ tbsp Gruyere Cheese

1 Onion, spiralized

½ cup Vegetable Broth

Directions:

1. Preheat your oven to 400 degrees F.
2. Heat the live oil in a pan over medium heat, and cook the onion for about 5 minutes.
3. Add garlic and cook for one more minute.
4. Add the broth, season with salt and pepper, and cook for 5 more minutes.
5. Spray a baking dish (preferably a 9x13-inch one) with cooking spray, and arrange half of the spiralized potatoes, making an even layer.
6. Add half of the onion mixture over, and top with half of the gruyere cheese.
7. Repeat the process one more time, and top with parmesan cheese.
8. Cover the dish with alumnium foil and cook for 60 minutes.

Sweet and Cheesy Carrot Crostini

Serves: 6 \ Ready in: 25 minutes

Nutritional Info:

Calories 154.9, Carbohydrates 29 g, Fat 2.5 g, Protein 4.8 g

Ingredients:

1 Large Carrot, spiralized

2 tbsp Honey

¼ cup Maple Syrup

Pinch of Sea Salt

½ cup Ricotta Cheese

6 slices of White Bread

Directions:

1. Preheat your oven to 425 degrees F.
2. Line a cookie sheet with parchment paper and arrange the carrot noodles in an even layer.
3. Brush the noodles with maple syrup and sprinkle the sea salt over.
4. Bake for about 18 minutes, turning them over halfway through.
5. Divide the ricotta cheese between the crostini.
6. Top with carrot noodles.

Meatball Potato Cups

Serves: 6 \ Ready in: 45 minutes

Nutritional Info:

Calories 136, Carbohydrates 8 g, Fat 9 g, Protein 7 g

Ingredients:

1 tbsp Olvei Oil

2 Eggs, beaten

2 Large Potatoes, spiralized

6 frozen and pre-cooked Meatballs, defrosted

¾ cup Tomato Sauce

½ tsp Garlic Powder

Salt and Pepper, to taste

Directions:

1. Preheat your oven to 425 degrees F. Spray a muffin tin with cooking spray.
2. Heat the olive oil in a skillet over medium heat.
3. Add the potatoes, season with salt, pepper, and the garlic powder, and cook for 8 minutes.
4. Transfer the potatoes to a bowl, and let cool for about 2 minutes, until safe to handle.
5. Add the eggs in the bowl, and mix to combine.
6. Divide the potato mixture between the muffin cups.
7. Do your best to make a whole in each of these cups.
8. Place the meatballs in the holes.
9. Bake the potato cups for 15 minutes.
10. Meanwhile, place the tomato sauce in a saucepan over medium heat, and let simmer while the potato cups are in the oven.
11. Serve the potato cups topped with the tomato sauce.

Baked Mummies

Serves: 3 \ Ready in: 55 minutes

Nutritional Info:

Calories 167, Carbohydrates 25 g, Fat 6 g, Protein 4 g

Ingredients:

3 large Carrots

2 Large Potatoes, spiralized with the angel Hair Blade

1 tsp Goat Cheese

2 Black Olives

1 tbsp Olive Oil

Directions:

1. Preheat your oven to 450 degrees F. Line a baking sheet with waxed paper.
2. Bake the carrots for 10 minutes. Wrap the potato noodles around the carrots, making mummies. Brush them with the olive oil.
3. Place in the oven and bake for 30 minutes. Slice the olives and place 2 small olive slices on the mummies.
4. These will be the eyes. Top the eyes with dabs of goat cheese.

Rutabaga Chips

Serves: 2 \ Ready in: 45 minutes

Nutritional Info:

Calories 133.8, Carbohydrates 16.7 g, Fat 7.1 g, Protein 2.6 g

Ingredients:

1 Medium Rutabaga, spiralized with the straight blade

1 tsp Garlic Powder

1 tbsp Olive Oil

Directions:

1. Preheat your oven to 375 degrees F.
2. Line a baking sheet with parchment paper.
3. Place all of the ingredients in a bowl and toss to combine.
4. Arrange the chips on the baking sheet.
5. Bake for 35 minutes, turning over halfway through.

Turmeric Veggie Fritters

Serves: 5 \ Ready in: 17 minutes

Nutritional Info:

Calories 152, Carbohydrates 20 g, Fat 7 g, Protein 5 g

Ingredients:

1 large Zucchini, spiralized

1 large Carrot, spiralized

¾ cup Corn Meal

2 Eggs, beaten

2 tbsp Olive Oil

1 tsp Turmeric

5 Scallions, chopped

Directions:

1. Place zucchini, corn meal, eggs, carrots, scallions, and turmeric, in a large bowl.
2. Mix with your hands until fully combined.
3. Make 5 patties out of the mixture.
4. Heat the olive oil in a large skillet.
5. Fry the fritter for about 2-3 minutes per side.

Sweet Potato and Marshmallow Bited

Serves: 3 \ Ready in: 40 minutes

Nutritional Info:

Calories 138.4, Carbohydrates 22.3 g, Fat 4.1 g, Protein 3.2 g

Ingredients:

½ cup Mini Marshmallows

½ tbsp Olive Oil

1 Large Sweet Potato, spiralized

¼ tsp Nutmeg

1 Egg

Directions:

1. Spray a skillet with cooking spray, add the potatoes and nutmeg, and cook for about 7 minutes.
2. Transfer them to a bowl, and wait for about 2 minutes, until easy to handle.
3. Crack the egg in the bowl, and mix with your hand.
4. Divide the mixture between 3 bigger ramekins.
5. Top them with a piece of parchment paper, and place something heavy on top of the potatoes. A can will do just fine.
6. Place the ramekins in the fridge for 15 minutes.
7. Heat the olive oil in a skillet.
8. Cook the potato buns for about 3 minutes on both sides.
9. Place them on a lined baking dish and top with marshmallow.
10. Bake in the oven at medium heat, for about 2 minutes, or until the marshmallow become slightly browned.
11. Slice into bite-sized pieces and serve with toothpicks.

Baked Fries with Cheese and Garlic

Serves: 4 \ Ready in: 35 minutes

Nutritional Info:

Calories 159, Carbohydrates 15 g, Fat 10 g, Protein 4 g

Ingredients:

1 Sweet Potato, spiralized

1 Idaho Potato, spiralized

⅓ cup grated Asiago Cheese

1 tbsp Garlic Powder

2 tbsp Olive Oil

Directions:

1. Preheat your oven to 450 degrees F. Combine all of the ingredients in a large bowl. Place the noodles on a lined baking sheet.
2. Bake for about 15 minutes, flipping over once.

Cheese Stuffed Plantain Balls

Serves: 4 \ Ready in: 30 minutes

Nutritional Info:

Calories 146.8, Carbohydrates 22.2 g, Fat 5.6 g, Protein 4.2 g

Ingredients:

2 Plantains, peeled and spiralized

½ ounce Coconut Flakes

5 tbsp Goat Cheese

1 slice of Whole Wheat Bread Toast

1 Egg, beaten

Directions:

1. Preheat your oven to 400 degrees F.
2. Place the toast in a food processor and process until crumbled.
3. Place the plantain noodles in the food processor and process until 'rice' is made.
4. Coat a skillet with cooking spray and cook the plantain rice until browned.
5. Transfer to a bowl, along with the rest of the ingredients, except the cheese.
6. Make balls out of the mixture.
7. Line a baking sheet with parchment paper and flatten the balls on it.
8. Add goat cheese in the middle, and re-roll into balls.
9. Bake for about 15 minutes.

Prosciutto-Wrapped Potatoes with Pecans

Serves: 12 \ Ready in: 20 minutes

Nutritional Info:

Calories 167, Carbohydrates 17 g, Fat 8 g, Protein 10 g

Ingredients:

1 large Sweet Potato, spiralized

12 Prosciutto slices, cut in half

2 tsp Dijon Mustard

¼ cup Maple Syrup

6 Fates, sliced

3 tbsp Goat Cheese

1 tbsp Olive Oil

3 tbsp Balsamic Vinegar

½ cup chopped Pecans

Directions:

1. Heat the olive oil in a skillet over medium heat. Add the potato noodles and cook for about 7 minutes.
2. Meanwhile, whisk together the vinegar and maple syrup in a saucepan.
3. Place over medium heat and cook for about 5 minutes. Stir in the mustard.
4. On a flat surface, lay out 2 slices of prosciutto.
5. Smear them with about half a tablespoon of cheese.
6. Add sliced dates and pecans.
7. Top with potato noodles.
8. Roll to wrap everything.
9. Slice the wraps in half, and use toothpicks to secure.
10. Repeat with the remaining ingredients.
11. Serve drizzled with the maple glaze and enjoy.

Parsnip Gratin with Kale

Serves: 4 \ Ready in: 20 minutes

Nutritional Info:

Calories 391, Carbohydrates 36g, Fat 20 g, Protein 19 g

Ingredients:

4 Large Parsnips, spiralized with the straight blade

2 Garlic Cloves, minced

1 tbsp Olive Oil

3 cups shredded Gouda

2 ½ tsp Thyme

¼ tsp Red Pepper Flakes

6 cups Kale, packed

Directions:

1. Preheat your oven to 425 degrees F.
2. Spray a baking dish (preferably a 9x13-inch one) with cooking spray.
3. Heat the olive oil in a skillet and add garlic, thyme, and red pepper flakes.
4. Cook for 30 seconds.
5. Add the kale and cook for 4 more minutes.
6. Arrange a single layer of a third of the parsnip noodles, top with ⅓ of the kale, and sprinkle 1 cup of Gouda cheese.
7. Repeat the process two more times.
8. Cover the dish with foil and bake for 30 minutes.

RICE AND RISOTTO

Garlicky Squash Risotto with Leeks

Serves: 4 \ Ready in: 45 minutes

Nutritional Info:

Calories 124, Carbohydrates 12 g, Fat 6 g, Protein 5 g

Ingredients:

⅓ cup grated Parmesan Cheese

1 medium Squash, spiralized

¾ cup sliced Leeks

½ cup Chicken Broth

½ tsp Thyme

1 tbsp Olive Oil

Directions:

1. Place the squash noodles in your food processor and pulse until rice is made.
2. Heat the olive oil in a skillet over medium heat and cook the leeks and garlic for 5 minutes.
3. Stir in the rice and thyme and cook for 2 more minutes.
4. Pour the broth over and bring the mixture to a boil.
5. Reduce the heat and cook for 15 minutes.
6. Stir in the parmesan cheese.

Salmon with Potato Rice

Serves: 1 \ Ready in: 35 minutes

Nutritional Info:

Calories 297, Carbohydrates 28 g, Fat 9 g, Protein 26 g

Ingredients:

1 Garlic Clove, minced

1 tsp chopped Cilantro

1 smallish Sweet Potato, spiralized

½ tbsp Olive Oil

1 Lemon, sliced

1 cup Baby Spinach

14 ounces Salmon Fillet, skinless

Directions:

1. Preheat your oven to 415 degrees F.
2. Place the potato noodles in a food processor and pulse until rice is formed.
3. Transfer to a bowl.
4. Stir in garlic and cilantro.
5. Place the mixture in the middle of a 10x10 piece of alumnium foil, and top with spinach.
6. Place the salmon on top and drizzle the olive oil over.
7. Arrange the lemon slices over.
8. Fold the foil and secure the top.
9. Place in a baking dish and cook for about 25 minutes.

Pork Butt with Turnip Rice

Serves: 5 \ Ready in: 3 hours and 25 minutes

Nutritional Info:

Calories 308, Carbohydrates 14 g, Fat 19 g, Protein 20 g

Ingredients:

1 pound Pork Butt, cut into 3-inch long pieces

3 large Turnips, spiralzied

2 Eggs, beaten

1 small Onion, diced

4 Scallions, diced

1 tbsp Tamari Sauce

½ tbsp Olive Oil

¼ tsp White Pepper

Marinade:

½ tbsp Olive Oil

1 tsp Hoisin Sauce

½ tsp Salt

½ tbsp Sherry

1 tsp Tomato Paste

½ tbsp Honey

2 Garlic Cloves, minced

¼ tsp Five Spice Powder

½ tsp Paprika

½ tbsp Hot Water

Directions:

1. Whisk the marinade ingredients together in a bowl.
2. Set 2 tbsp of the marinade aside, and add the rest in a Zip Loc bag.
3. Add the pork in the Zip Loc bag, shake to coat well, and refrigerate fo 2 hours.
4. Preheat the oven to 375 degrees F.
5. Roast the meat for 25 minutes.
6. Turn over and roast for another 20 minutes.
7. Brush the rest of the marinade over the pork and let sit for 10 minutes. Cut into smaller pieces.
8. Meanwhile, place the turnips in a food processor and process until rice is formed.
9. Coat a skillet with cooking spray, place over medium heat, add the eggs, scramble and cook until set. Set aside.
10. Heat the olive oil and cook the onions for 3 minutes.
11. Add rice and pork, and cook for 5 more minutes.
12. Stir in the rest of the ingredients, along with the eggs, and cook for 2 more minutes.

Saffron Veggie Paella with Carrot Rice

Serves: \ Ready in: 20 minutes

Nutritional Info:

Calories 138, Carbohydrates 19 g, Fat 5 g, Protein 5 g

Ingredients:

3 Large Carrots, spiralized

1 Red Bell Pepper, spiralized

14 ounces canned Tomatoes

1 Onion, diced

½ tsp Cayenne Pepper

2 cups Broccoli Florets

1 cup Frozen Peas

14 ounces artichoke Heatrs, quartered

1 tsp Saffron Threads

1 tbsp Olive Oil

1 tbsp minced Garlic

1 ½ tsp Paprika

1 ½ tsp Smoked Paprika

1 tbsp chopped Cilantro

½ cup chopped Olives

½ cup Veggie Broth

Directions:

1. Place the carrot noodles in the food processor nad pulse until rice is formed.
2. Heat the olive oil in a skillet and cook the onion and garlic for 3 minutes. Stir in cayenne pepper, saffron, and paprika.
3. Add bell pepper noodles and broccoli, and cook for 3 minutes. Stir in the rest of the ingredients and cook for 10 minutes.

Bacon and Walnut Zucchini Risotto in Sweet Dressing

Serves: 2 \ Ready in: 20 minutes

Nutritional Info:

Calories 346, Carbohydrates 31 g, Fat 23 g, Protein 10 g

Ingredients:

1 Large Zucchini, spiralized

⅓ cup chopped Walnuts

¼ cup dried Cranberries

4 Bacon Strips

1 ounce Goat Cheese

1 ½ tbsp Apple Cider Vinegar

¾ tsp Dijon Mustard

1 ½ tbsp Maple Syrup

½ tbsp Olive Oil

Directions:

1. Pulse the zoodles in a food processor to make rice. Heat a skillet over medium heat and cook the bacon until crispy. Set aside.
2. Add the zucchini rice and cook for about 1 minutes. Transfer to a bowl.
3. In a small bowl, whisk together vinegar, maple, mustard and olive oil.
4. Add the bacon, goat cheese, walnuts, and cranberries to the bowl with rice.
5. Mix to combine. Pour the dressing over.

Simple Thyme-Flavored Beet Risotto

Serves: 2 \ Ready in: 25 minutes

Nutritional Info:

Calories 272, Carbohydrates 13 g, Fat 22 g, Protein 9 g

Ingredients:

2 Large Beets, peeled and spiralized

⅓ cup chopped Walnuts

¼ cup Vegetable Broth

2 tbsp minced Shallots

1 tbsp Olive Oil

1 Garlic Cloves, minced

¼ cup grated Parmesan Cheese

1 tsp Thyme Leaves

Directions:

1. Place the noodles in your food processor and pulse until rice is formed.
2. Heat the olive oil in a skillet over medium heat and cook the garlic and shallots for 30 seconds.
3. Stir in the thyme and broth.
4. Bring the mixture to a boil, reduce the heat, and simmer for 7 minutes.
5. Stir in the parmesan cheese. Serve topped with walnuts.

Chicken and Mushroom Casserole with Celery Rice

Serves: 6 \ Ready in: 1 hour and 30 minutes

Nutritional Info:

Calories 191, Carbohydrates 9 g, Fat 9 g, Protein 18 g

Ingredients:

2 Chicken Breasts, boneless and skinless

1 Large Celery Root, spiralized

1 cup Chicken Broth

8 ounces Baby Mushrooms, quartered

3 Eggs

2 Garlic Cloves, minced

2 tbsp Olive Oil

1 Onion, diced

½ tsp Nutmeg

10 ounces Spinach

½ tsp Nutmeg

13 ounces Coconut Milk

Directions:

1. Preheat your oven to 325 degrees F. Pulse the celeriac noodles in your food processor until rice is formed. Place them in a baking dish, in an even layer.

2. Heat half of the oil in a skillet over medium heat.

3. Cook the chicken until no longer pink, about 7 minutes. Set aside.

4. Heat the rest of the oil and cook the onion for 5 minutes.

5. Add garlic and cook for 300 more minutes.

6. Stir in mushrooms and cook for another 5 minutes.

7. Finally, add spinach, and cook for 3 minutes.

8. In a bowl, whisk together the eggs, broth, nutmeg, and milk.

9. Place the veggies and chicken on top of the celeriac noodles.

10. Pour the egg mixture over. Bake for about 50 minutes.

Spicy Sausage and Carrot Risotto

Serves: 2 \ Ready in: 25 minutes

Nutritional Info:

Calories 217, Carbohydrates 10 g, Fat 18 g, Protein 9 g

Ingredients:

1 large Carrot, spiralized

3 tsp diced Jalapeno

Juice of 1 Lime

2 spicy Sausages

1 tbsp Olive Oil

½ tsp Chili Powder

½ cup Chicken Broth

1 tbsp chopped Cilantro

½ Avocado, sliced

Directions:

1. Pulse the carrot noodles in your food processor until rice is formed.
2. Heat the olive oil in a skillet over medium heat.
3. Cook the sausage while breaking it with a wooden spoon, for about 3 minutes.
4. Stir in the rice, cilantro, lime juice, broth, jalapenos, and chili powder.
5. Cook for about 10 minutes. Serve topped with avocado.

Golden Beet Risotto with Peas, Corn, and Peppers

Serves: 2 \ Ready in: 30 minutes

Nutritional Info:

Calories 248, Carbohydrates 29 g, Fat 7 g, Protein 12 g

Ingredients:

3 medium Golden Beets, peeled and spiralized

2 Scallions, diced

2 Eggs, beaten

¼ cup canned Corn

½ cup frozen Peas

2 Garlic Cloves, minced

1 tsp Olive Oil

½ cup diced Bell Peppers

1 tsp Tamari Sauce

Directions:

1. Place the beet noodles in the food processor and pulse to form rice.
2. Heat the oil in a skillet and cook the bell peppers, scallions, and garlic, for about 3 minutes.

3. Add the beet rice and cook for 2 more minutes.
4. Crack the eggs into the skillet, scramble them, and add peas, corn, and tamari. Cook for a couple of minutes, until the peas are softened.

Kohlrabi Scallop Risotto

Serves: 1 \ Ready in: 35 minutes

Nutritional Info:

Calories 414, Carbohydrates 18 g, Fat 22 g, Protein 40 g

Ingredients:

1 ½ tbsp Olive Ol

6 Jumbo Scallops

3 tbsp grated Parmesan Cheese

1 Garlic Clove, minced

1 Large Kohlrabi, spiralized

½ cup minced Onion

1 ½ cups Spinach

¼ cup Veggie Broth

Juice and Zest of ½ Lemon

Directions:

1. Place the noodles in the food processor and pulse to make rice.
2. Heat 1 tbsp olive oil in a skillet. Cook the onions and garlic for 3 minutes.
3. Add spinach and cook for 2 more minutes. Stir in rice and cook for one minute.
4. Pour in the broth and cook for 5 minutes. Transfer to a serving bowl.
5. Heat the remaining olive oil and cook the scallops for about 2 minutes per side.
6. Add the scallops on top of the risotto. Sprinkle the cheese over.

Bacon and Onion Squash Rice

Serves: 2 \ Ready in: 40 minutes

Nutritional Info:

Calories 280, Carbohydrates 34 g, Fat 10 g, Protein 14 g

Ingredients:

4 Bacon Slices

1 Butternut Squash, spiralized

½ tsp Paprika

¼ cup Chicken Broth

2 Hard boiled Eggs

½ Red Onion, spiralized

¼ tsp Garlic Powder

Directions:

1. Pulse the squash in a food processor to make rice.
2. Cook the oil in a preheated skillet and cook over medium heat until crispy. Transfer to a plate.
3. Add the onions and cook until caramelized, about 10 minutes.
4. Stir in the rice, paprika, and garlic powder.
5. After 1 minutes, pour in the broth, and cook for 7 minutes.
6. Serve topped with crumbled bacon and grated hard boiled eggs.

Creamy Rutabaga and Chicken Rice

Serves: 2 \ Ready in: 20 minutes

Nutritional Info:

Calories 358, Carbohydrates 35.7 g, Fat 15.6 g, Protein 21.7 g

Ingredients:

1 Large Rutabaga, spiralized

1 tsp Thyme

3 tbsp Parmesan Cheese

4 ounces cooked and shredded Chicken Breast

⅓ cup chopped Onions

1 Garlic Clove, minced

¼ cup Heavy Cream

½ tbsp Olive Oil

¼ cup Water

Directions:

1. Pulse the rutabaga noes in a food processor to make rice.
2. Heat the olive oil in a skillet over medium heat.
3. Add onions and cook for 3 minutes.
4. Add the garlic and cook for 30 more seconds.
5. Stir in thyme, and rice and cook for 1 minute.
6. Add water and heavy cream and cook for 6 more minutes.
7. Stir in chicken and parmesan cheese.

PASTA

Lean Zoodle Bolognese with Turkey

Serves: 4 \ Ready in: 30 minutes

Nutritional Info:

Calories 369, Carbohydrates 22 g, Fat 14 g, Protein 40 g

Ingredients:

2 Celery Stalks, diced

2 Garlic cloves, minced

1 pound Lean Turkey, ground

4 Large Zucchinis, spiralized

24 ounces Tomato Sauce

2 ½ tsp Oregano lakes

1 tbsp Olive Oil

2 Carrots, diced

½ Red Onion, diced

Directions:

1. Heat te oil in a skillet over medium heat.
2. Add onions and celery and cook for 3 minutes
3. Add garlic and cook for 30 seconds.
4. Push the veggies to the side, add the turkey, and cook until browned.
5. Stir in oregano.
6. Pour the tomato sauce over and cook for 5 minutes.
7. Add the zoodles and cook for 5 more minutes.

Quick Squash Pasta with Lemon and Basil

Serves: 2 \ Ready in: 10 minutes

Nutritional Info:

Calories 97, Carbohydrates 12 g, Fat 6 g, Protein 3 g

Ingredients:

3 large Yello Summer Squash, spiralized

2 tsp olive Oil

1 tsp chopped Mint

1 tbsp chopped Basil

1 Celery Stalk, diced

¼ tsp Cumin

2 tsp Lemon Juice

½ tsp Lemon Zest

Salt and Pepper, to taste

Directions:

1. Place all of the ingredients in a large bowl.
2. Season with salt and pepper. Mix to combine well.

Veggie Pasta with Sausages

Serves: 4 \ Ready in: 45 minutes

Nutritional Info:

Calories 196, Carbohydrates 17 g, Fat 10 g, Protein 11 g

Ingredients:

3 Garlic Cloves, minced

2 Bell Eppeprs, spiralized

2 Large Russet Potatoes, spiralized

1 Large Red Onion, spiralized

2 tbsp Olive Oil

1 tsp Oregano

¼ tsp Red Pepper Flakes

4 Italian Sausage Links

1 tsp Basil

Directions:

1. Preheat the oven to 425 degrees F.
2. Bake the sausage in a baking dish for about 25 minutes.
3. Meanwhile, in a skillet over medium heat, heat the olive oil.
4. Add the noodles along with the seasonings. Stir to combine and cook for 15 minutes.
5. Slice the sausages and stir into the pasta mixture.

Squash Spaghetti with Chicken and Broccoli

Serves: 4 \ Ready in: 35 minutes

Nutritional Info:

Calories 319, Carbohydrates 27 g, Fat 15 g, Protein 24 g

Ingredients:

3 cups Broccoli Florets

1 Large Butternut Squash, spiralized

2 Chicken Breasts, cubed

1 tbsp Olive Oil

1 Garlic Clove, minced

½ tsp Salt

bsp Nutritional Yeast

2 tsp Lemon Juice

1 tbsp minced Shallors

¾ cup Cashews

½ cup Veggie Brith

Directions:

1. Preheat your oven to 400 degrees F.
2. Arrange the noodles on a lined baking sheet and bake for 12 minutes.
3. Meanwhile, heat the oil in a skillet, and cook the chicken until no longer pink.
4. Add broccoli and cook for 4 more minutes.
5. Place the salt, garlic, lemon juice, shallots, cashews, yeast, and veggie broth, in a food processor.Pulse until smooth.
6. Add the pasta to the skillet with the chicken, pour the sauce over, and stir to combine.

Bell Pepper Beef Pasta

Serves: 3 \ Ready in: 40 minutes

Nutritional Info:

Calories 447, Carbohydrates 19 g, Fat 26 g, Protein 33 g

Ingredients:

1 tbsp Olive Oil

½ tsp dried Oregano

½ cup canned Tomato Sauce

2 Green Bell Peppers, spiralized

½ tsp Cumin

3 tbsp golden Raisisns

¼ cup quartered Olives

½ cup chopped Onions

¾ pound ground Beef

2 Garlic Cloves, minced

Directions:

1. Heat the oil in a skillet and cook the pepper noodles until al dente, about 5 minutes. Transfer to a bowl.
2. Add the garlic and onions to the skillet, and cook for 5 minutes.
3. Add beef and cook until browned, abut 10 minutes.
4. Stir in the rest of the ingredients.
5. Serve the sauce over the bell pepper noodles.

Lemony Tuna Zucchini Pasta

Serves: 2 \ Ready in: 20 minutes

Nutritional Info:

Calories 286, Carbohydrates 16 g, Fat 21 g, Protein 12 g

Ingredients:

2 tbsp Olive Oil

2 medium Zucchinis, spiralized

3 ounces Canned Tuna

1 tbsp chopped Parsley

Juce and Zest from ½ Lemon

⅛ tsp Red Pepper Flakes

1 Garlic Clove, minced

¼ cup chopped Kalamata Olives

Directions:

1. Heat the oil in a skillet and cook the garlic for 30 seconds.
2. Add zoodles and cook for 5 minutes. Stir in the rest of the ingredients.

Lamb and Celeriac Pasta

Serves: 3 \ Ready in: 60 minutes

Nutritional Info:

Calories 429, Carbohydrates 19 g, Fat 24 g, Protein 34 g

Ingredients:

1 Garlic Clove, minced

¾ pound Ground Lamb

½ Carrot, diced

14 ounces canned crushed Tomatoes

½ tsp chopped Rosemary

1 Celeriac, spiralized

½ tbsp Tomato Paste

½ tsp Thyme

½ cup Chicken Broth

½ tbso Olive Oil

1 tbsp chopped Mint

½ Onion, chopped

½ Celery Stalk, diced

Directions:

1. Grease a pot with cooking spray and add the lamb, garlic, cumin, thyme, and rosemary. Cook until the lamb turns brown.
2. Add carrots, onion, celery, red pepper flakes, and cook for 5 more minutes.
3. Add the tomato paste, tomato, and broth.
4. Bring to a boil, then reduce the heat, and let dimmer for 25 minutes.
5. Heat the olive oil in a skillet over medium heat.
6. Add celery noodles and cook for about 5-10 minutes.
7. Serve the pasta topped with the lamb sauce.

Pesto and Kale Beet Pasta

Serves: 3 \ Ready in: 25 minutes

Nutritional Info:

Calories 263, Carbohydrates 10 g, Fat 25 g, Protein 3 g

Ingredients:

2 Beets, spiralized

2 cups Kale

½ tbsp Olive Oil

Pesto:

¼ cup Olive Oil

3 cups Basil Leaves

½ tsp Sea Slt

1 Garlic Clove, minced

¼ tsp Pepper

¼ cup Pine Nuts

Directions:

1. Preheat the oven to 425 degrees F.
2. Arrange the beet noodles on a lined baking dish and drizzle the oil over.
3. Bake for 5-10 minutes.
4. Place all of the pesto ingredients in a food processor and pulse until smooth.
5. Combine the noodles and pesto. Stir in the kale.

Pomodoro Zoodles

Serves: 3 \ Ready in: 25 minutes

Nutritional Info:

Calories 238, Carbohydrates 30 g, Fat 7 g, Protein 5 g

Ingredients:

2 ¼ cups Spiralized Zucchini

14 ounces crushed Tomatoes

½ cup diced Onion

½ tbsp minced Garlic

1 ½ tbsp chopped Basil

1 tbsp Olive Oil

Directions:

1. Heat the oil in a skillet andcook the garlic until fragrant.
2. Add onions and cook for 2 minutes. Stir in the tomatoes and basil.
3. Cook for about 6 minutes. Stir in the zoodles and cook for 5 more minutes.

Broccoli Spaghetti with Chicken and Chickpeas

Serves: 3 \ Ready in: 35 minutes

Nutritional Info:

Calories 399, Carbohydrates 29 g, Fat 14 g, Protein 39 g

Ingredients:

2 Broccoli Stems, spiralized

½ cup sliced Leeks

¾ pound Chicken Breasts, cut into cubes

½ cup canned Chickpeas

½ cup canned Peas

½ tbsp Olive Oil

¼ tsp Oregano

Dressing:

1 tbsp Lemon Juice

½ chopped shallot

⅓ cup crumbled Feta

1 tbsp Red Wine Vinegar

2 tbsp chopped Basil

1 Garlic Clove, minced

1 tbsp Olive Oil

Directions:

1. Heat the oil in a skillet and add chicken and oregano.
2. Cook until no longer pink.
3. Place a pot with water over medium heat and bring to a boil.
4. Add broccoli and cook for 2 minutes.
5. Place all of the dressing ingredients in a food processor and pulse until smooth.
6. In a large bowl, add spaghetti, chickpeas, chicken, peas, leeks, and pour over the dressing. Mix to combine.

Pasta Primavera

Serves: 3 \ Ready in: 35 minutes

Nutritional Info:

Calories 224, Carbohydrates 25 g, Fat 10 g, Protein 14 g

Ingredients:

1 ½ cups Broccoli Florets

2 Medium Zucchini, spiralized

½ cup Green Peas

3 tsp minced Garlic

1 tbsp Olive Oil

¼ tsp Red Pepper Flakes

1 cup halved Cherry Tomatoes

1 Bell Pepepr, sliced

2 tbsp Lemon Juice

2 Carrots, shaved

½ cup grated Parmesan Cheese

2 tbsp chopped Parsley

½ Red Onion, sliced

Directions:

1. Bring a pot filled with water to a boil over medium heat.
2. Add broccoli and cook for 2 minutes. Drain and set aside.
3. Heat the olive oil in a skillet and add the onions, garlic, and red pepper flakes.
4. Cook for 3 minutes. Add peas, bell peppers, nad cherry tomatoes, and cook for 3 minutes.
5. Stir in zoodles, carrot, parsley, and lemon juice, and cook for 3 more minutes.
6. Stir in broccoli and parmesan cheese.

Shrimp and Tomato Zucchini Spaghetti

Serves: 1 \ Ready in: 20 minutes

Nutritional Info:

Calories 287, Carbohydrates 32 g, Fat 15 g, Protein 5.57 g

Ingredients:

1 ½ Zucchinis, spiralized

¾ can (14-ounce one) diced Tomatoes

1 tsp Red Pepper Flakes

1 tbsp Oreano

1 ½ cup chopped Kale

½ Onion, chopped

4 medium Shrimp, deveined and deshelled

1 Garlic Clove, minced

1 tbsp Olive Oil

Directions:

1. Heat the olive oil and cook onions for 3 minutes.
2. Add garlic and red pepper flakes and cook for 30 seconds.
3. Stir in tomatoes and oregano, and cook for 10 minutes.
4. Stir in kale and zoodles.
5. Coat another skillet with cooking spray.
6. Cook shrimp over medium heat for about 2 minutes per side.
7. Serve shrimp on top of the pasta.

Baked Cheesy Rutabaga Spaghetti

Serves: 6 \ Ready in: 1 hour and 10 minutes

Nutritional Info:

Calories 282, Carbohydrates 24 g, Fat 14 g, Protein 16 g

Ingredients:

28 ounces canned peeled Tomatoes

2 Medium Rutabagas, spiralized

2 Garlic Cloves, minced

2 cups Basil Leaves

9 slices of Mozzarella Cheese

1 tbsp Olive Oil

Salt and Pepper, to taste

Directions:

1. Preheat your oven to 400 degrees F.
2. Pulse tomatoes in a food processor.
3. Heat the olive oil in a skillet and cook the rutabaga seasoned with salt and pepper, about 15 minutes.
4. Transfer to a bowl.
5. Coat the skillet with cooking spray and add garlic.
6. Cook for 30 seconds.
7. Add the tomatoes and let simmer for 15 minutes.
8. Add the tomatoes and basil in the bowl with spaghetti and mix to combine.
9. Coat a baking dish and arrange the spaghetti in an even layer.
10. Top with mozzarella. Bake for 25 minutes.

Potato Carbonara with Chickpeas

Serves: 2 \ Ready in: 20 minutes

Nutritional Info:

Calories 470, Carbohydrates 49 g, Fat 18 g, Protein 29 g

Ingredients:

4 Bacon Slices

½ cup canned Chickpeas, drained and rinsed

2 Eggs

⅛ cup Parmesan Cheese

¼ tsp Onion Powder

1 Large Sweet Potato, spiralized

2 tbsp minced Shallots

¼ tsp Chili Powder

⅛ tsp Red Pepper Flakes

2 Garlic Cloves, minced

¼ tsp Paprika

Directions:

1. Heat a skillet over medium heat and cook the bacon until crispy. Set aside.
2. Add shallots and garlic and cook for 1-2 minutes.
3. Add noodles and cook for 7 minutes. Set aside.
4. Coat the skillet with cooking spray and add the chickpeas.
5. Cook for 5 minutes, until slightly browned. Whisk the eggs and combine with the parmesan cheese.
6. Place all of the ingredients in the skillet, crumble the bacon, and pour the egg mixture over.
7. Cook for 2 minutes stirring constantly.

Simple Pesto and Asparagus Zoodles

Serves: 2 \ Ready in: 17 minutes

Nutritional Info:

Calories 311, Carbohydrates 13 g, Fat 27 g, Protein 8 g

Ingredients:

1 tsp Olive Oil

¼ cup Pesto Sauce (store-bought or homemade)

4 thick Asparagus Spears, sliced

2 Zucchinis, spiralized

Salt and Pepper, to taste

Directions:

1. Heat the oil in a skillet, add asparagus, and season with salt and pepper.
2. Cook for 5 minutes.
3. Add zucchini and cook for 2 more minutes.
4. Stir in the pesto sauce.
5. Serve and enjoy!

DESSERTS

Chocolate Zucchini Muffins

Serves: 12 \ Ready in: 45 minutes

Nutritional Info:

Calories 118, Carbohydrates 14 g, Fat 5 g, Protein 4 g

Ingredients:

½ cup Coconut Flour

3 Eggs

1 Banana, mashed

¾ tsp Baking Soda

2 tsp Cinnamon

½ tsp Nutmeg

3 tbsp Almond Milk

1 tbsp Cacao Powder

1 Zucchini, spiralized and chopped

⅓ cup Chocolate Chips

3 tbsp Maple Syrup

1 tbsp Butter or Coconut Oil

2 tsp Vanilla Extract

Directions:

1. Preheat your oven to 350 degrees F. Grease your muffin tin with cooking spray. Combine the dry ingredients in one bowl and whisk the wet ones in another.
2. Combine the two mixtures gently. Stir in zucchini and chocolate chips.
3. Pour the batter into the muffin cups. Bake for 30 minutes.

Coconut Frosted Carrot Muffins

Serves: 12 \ Ready in: 40 minutes

Nutritional Info:

Calories 181, Carbohydrates 21 g, Fat 13 g, Protein 3 g

Ingredients:

4 Eggs

1 tsp Baking Powder

¼ cup melted butter

8 Dates, pitted and chopped

1 large Carrot, spiralized and chopped

1 tsp Vanilla Extract

Pinch of Salt

½ cup Coconut or Almond Flour

½ tsp Nutmeg

2 tsp Cinnamon

Frosting:

14 ounces Coconut Milk

1 tsp Vanilla Extract

1 tbsp Maple Syrup

Directions:

1. Preheat your oven to 350 degrees F and grease a muffin tin.
2. Combine the butter and dates in a food processor. Pulse until smooth. Add eggs and vanilla, and pulse until combined.
3. In another bowl combine the dry ingredients, and gently stir the mixture into the one in the food processor. Stir in carrots.
4. Divide the batter between the muffin cups and bake for 27 minutes. Let them cool. Meanwhile, beat together the frosting ingredients. Frost the muffins.

Chocolate Covered Apple Strings

Serves: 12 \ Ready in: 3 hours and 15 minutes

Nutritional Info:

Calories 153, Carbohydrates 21 g, Fat 8 g, Protein 16 g

Ingredients:

3 Apples, spiralized

10 ounces Chocolate Chips, melted

Toppings by choice (nuts, coconut, sprinkles, etc.)

Directions:

1. Line a baking sheet with parchment paper. Arrange the apple string on the dish. Pour the melted chocolate over.

2. Top with desired toppings, if using any. Freeze for about 3 hours.

Pear and Almond Tart

Serves: 8 \ Ready in: 37 minutes

Nutritional Info:

Calories 234, Carbohydrates 24 g, Fat 14 g, Protein 5.6 g

Ingredients:

1 ¼ cups Almond Meal

1 Egg, beaten

¼ cup Maple Syrup

¼ cup Oat Flour

2 tbsp Butter or Coconut Oil, melted

¼ tsp Almond Extract

1 tsp Vanilla Extract

¼ tsp Sea Salt

16 ounces Spiralized Pears

1 tbsp Honey mixed with 2 tbsp Lemon

Juice, optional

Directions:

1. Preehat the oven to 350 degrees and coat a tart pan with cooking spray.
2. Combine flour, almond meal, and baking powder, in one bowl.
3. In another one, whisk together the wet ingrediens along with the salt.
4. Combine both mixtures gently. Pour the dough in the tart pan.
5. Top with spiralized apples. Drizzle the honey/lemon mixture if using.
6. Bake for 25 minutes.

Pumpkin and Ginger Cupcakes

Serves: \ Ready in: 1 hour and 30 minutes

Nutritional Info:

Calories 211, Carbohydrates 31.8 g, Fat 8.7 g, Protein 2.4 g

Ingredients:

2 cups Flour

¼ tsp ground Cloves

1 package instant Butterscotch Pudding

1 tbsp Cinnamon

½ tsp Allspice

2 tsp Baking Soda

½ tsp ginger

1 cup Butter

4 Eggs

15 ounces spiralized and chopped Pumpkin

1 cup White Sugar

1 cup Brown Sugar

⅓ cup chopped Crystallized Ginger

Directions:

1. Preheat your oven to 350 degrees, and grease 24 muffin tins.
2. In one bowl, combine the flour, ginger, allspice, cinnamon, cloves, baking soda,pudding mix, and crystalized ginger. In another one, beat together the butter with the sugars until fluffy.
3. Beat n the eggs, one at a time, along with the vanilla. Stir in the flour mixture. Stir in pumpkin.
4. Pour the batter into the muffin cups. Bake for about 20 minutes.

Chocolate Glazed Zucchini Donuts

Serves: \ Ready in: 30 minutes

Nutritional Info:

Calories 177, Carbohydrates 25 g, Fat 7 g, Protein 6 g

Ingredients:

1 Zucchini, spiralized and chopped

½ cup Flour, this recipe uses Coconut

3 tbsp Maple Syrup

2 tsp Vanilla Extract

1 ½ tbs Maple Syrup

2 tsp Cinnamon

2 tbsp Milk

3 Eggs

¼ tsp Salt

¼ cup Tapioca Flour

1 tbsp Butter or Coconut Milk

1 Banana, mashed

2 tbsp shredded Coconut

½ tsp Nutmeg

¼ cup Chocolate Chips

Directions:

1. Preheat your oven to 350 degrees F, and grease a donut pan.
2. Combine the dry ingredients in one bowl, and whisk the wet ones in another.
3. Combine the two mixtures gently. Stir in the zucchini. Pour the batter in to the donut cups. Bake for 30 minutes. Melt the chocolate chips in a microwave and drizzle the chocolate over the donuts.
4. Let cool completely before serving.

Moist Carrot Cake with Pineapple and Walnuts

Serves: 12 \ Ready in: 1 hour and 20 minutes

Nutritional Info:

Calories 569, Carbohydrates 59.4 g, Fat 35.7 g, Protein 5.9 g

Ingredients:

1 tsp Salt

4 Eggs

2 cups All-Purpose Flour

2 ½ tsp Cinnamon

1 ½ cups Vegetable Oil

8 ounces canned and crushed Pineapple

2 ¾ cup spiralized and chopped Carrots

1 ½ tsp Baking Soda}2 tsp Baking Powder

2 cups Sugar

¾ cup chopped Walnuts

1 cup Coconut Flakes

Directions:

1. Preheat the oven to 325 degrees F. Grease a 9x13 baking dish.
2. Combine the flour, salt, cinnamon, baking powder and soda, in a bowl.
3. In another bowl, whisk together the eggs, oil, and sugar.
4. Combine the two mixtures together. Stir in carrots, pineapple, walnuts, and coconut.
5. Pour the batter in the prepared dish. Bake for 35 minutes. Let cool before slicing.

Simple Rhubarb and Apple Crisp

Serves: 4 \ Ready in: 45 minutes

Nutritional Info:

Calories 125, Carbohydrates 24 g, Fat 3 g, Protein 2 g

Ingredients:

3 Rhubarb Stalks, cubed

3 Apples, spiralized

½ cup Granola of your Choice

Honey for drizzling

Directions:

1. Preheat your oven to 350 degrees F. Combine the rhubarb and apple noodles in a bowl. Pack the mixture into 4 ramekins.
2. Drizzle them with honey, place in the oven, and bake for 30 minutes.
3. Divide the granola between the ramekins, and bake for 5 more minutes.

Blueberry and Zucchini Cake

Serves: 24 \ Ready in: 1 hour and 45 minutes

Nutritional Info:

Calories 230, Carbohydrates 33, Fat 10 g, Protein 2.6 g

Ingredients:

2 ¼ cups White Sugar

2 cups spiralized and chopped Zucchini

3 tsp Vanilla Extract

3 Eggs, beaten

1 cup Vegetable Oil

3 tsp Vanilla Extract

1 tsp Salt

1 tbsp Cinnamon

1 pint Blueberries

¼ tsp Baking Soda

3 cups Flour

Directions:

1. Preheat your oven to 350 degrees F. Grease 4 mini loaf pans.
2. Beat together eggs, oil, vanilla, and sugar, in a bowl.
3. In another bowl, combine the dry ingredients.
4. Combine the two mixtures carefully, and then stir in the zucchini and blueberries.
5. Pour the batter into the prepared pans. Bake for about 50 minutes.
6. Let cool for about 15 minutes in the pans, and then invert the cakes onto the wire rack.

Granny Smith Dumplings

Serves: 16 \ Ready in: 1 hour and 5 minutes

Nutritional Info:

Calories 333, Carbohydrates 38.5 g, Fat 19 g, Protein 2.7 g

Ingredients:

2 Large Granny Smith Apples, spiralized and chopped

1 cup Butter

20 ounces Crescent Roll Dough

1 tsp Cinnamon

1 ½ cups White Sugar

1 12-ounce can of Mountain Dew

Directions:

1. Preheat your oven to 350 degrees F, and grease a 9x13-inch baking pan.
2. Roll out the crescent rolls on a flat and floured surface, and cut into triangles.
3. Divide the spiralized apples between the triangles, then roll them up an seal by pinching the ends.
4. Melt the butter in a saucepan over medium heat and add sugar and cinnamon.
5. Arrange the apple dumplings on the baking dish,
6. Pour the butter mixture over them first, and then pour the Mountain Drew.
7. Bake for 40 minutes.

CONCLUSION

Now that you know the secret to making the perfect veggie noodles and have 100 different uses for them, the next step is to try out all of these recipes, modify them to your liking, and even create your own delicacies.

Thank you and happy spiralizing!

Brandon Mitchell

Made in the USA
Middletown, DE
19 November 2018